LEARN TO Bake

LEARN TO Bake

35 easy and fun recipes for children aged 7 years+

CICO Kidz

This edition published in 2021 by CICO Books
An imprint of Ryland Peters & Small Ltd
20–21 Jockey's Fields
London WC1R 4BW
341 E 116th St
New York, NY 10029
www.rylandpeters.com

First published in 2012 as *My First Baking Book*

10 9 8 7 6 5 4 3 2 1

A CIP catalog record for this book is available from the Library of Congress and the British Library.

ISBN: 978 1 80065 058 9

Printed in China

Series consultant: Susan Akass
Editors: Susan Akass and Katie Hardwicke
Designer: Elizabeth Healey
Step artworks: Rachel Boulton
Animal artworks: Hannah George
Templates: Simon Roulstone
For photography and styling credits, see page 128.

Art director: Sally Powell
Head of production: Patricia Harrington
Publishing manager: Penny Craig
Publisher: Cindy Richards

- All spoon measurements are level unless otherwise specified.

- Both US cup sizes or imperial and metric measurements have been given. Use one set of measurements only and not a mixture of both.

- All eggs are US large (UK medium) unless otherwise stated. This book contains recipes made with raw eggs. It is prudent for more vulnerable people, such as pregnant and nursing mothers, babies and young children, invalids and the elderly, to avoid uncooked dishes made with eggs.

- Some of the recipes contain nuts and should not be consumed by anyone with a nut allergy.

- Ovens should be preheated to the specified temperatures. All ovens work slightly differently. We recommend using an oven thermometer and suggest you consult the maker's handbook for any special instructions, particularly if you are cooking in a fan-assisted oven, as you will need to adjust temperatures according to manufacturer's instructions.

CONTENTS

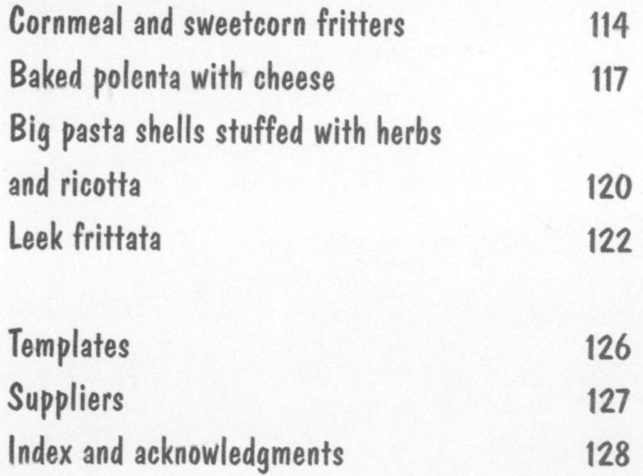

Introduction

Why learn to bake? There are three great reasons—it's lots of fun; you end up with delicious food to eat; and you create something special to share with your family and friends. What's more, it is a skill that will make you popular all through your life because everyone loves home-baked food.

This book teaches you how to bake by guiding you through each stage of a recipe, showing you how to do everything from greasing a pan to testing if a loaf is baked. It is divided into four chapters: the first, Perfect Pastry, is all about working with pastry to make mouth-watering savory and sweet pastry recipes. In the second chapter, Sweet Treats, you learn how to make cakes, bars, desserts, and cookies all guaranteed to bring your friends running. The third chapter, Delicious Dough, is all about using dough to make buns and bread-based recipes. Finally, Savory Meals and Snacks teaches you how to make some family meal dishes—your parents will be more than happy when you start offering to cook these for supper!

Obviously, you must ask an adult before doing any baking because using knives, stoves, ovens, and electrical equipment can be dangerous. However, the more you learn, the safer it will become. To help you, we have also included a techniques section with more detail about everything you will need to know to cook up the recipes.

We have also graded each recipe with a grading of one, two, or three smiley faces—see below. Level one recipes are the easiest, level two recipes have more stages, and level three recipes are the longest and most difficult—it may be best to leave these for when you have become more of an expert cook.

So, wash your hands, tie on your apron, and start baking!

Project levels

Level 1
These have only a few stages and require just a little adult help.

Level 2
These include more stages, some difficult techniques, and require some adult help.

Level 3
These are longer and require adult help for most of the stages.

Kitchen safety—read this before you start cooking!

- Always wash your hands before you start cooking and after touching raw meat.
- Tie long hair back so that it is out of the way.
- Wear an apron to keep your clothes clean.
- Make sure your ingredients are fresh and within their use-by date.
- When using sharp knives, electrical equipment, or the stovetop (hob), microwave, or oven, always ask an adult to help you.
- Use oven mitts when holding hot pans or dishes.
- Use a chopping board when using a sharp knife or metal cookie cutters— this protects the work surface and will help to stop the knife from slipping.
- Keep your work surface clean and wipe up any spills on the floor so that you don't slip.
- Don't forget to clear up afterward—washing the dishes can be as much fun as baking!

Kitchen equipment

Strainer (sieve)
Colander
Vegetable peeler
Grater
Garlic crusher
Sharp knives
Palette knife

Cutting board
Egg cup
Ovenproof dishes
Plastic wrap (clingfilm)
Baking parchment
Paper towel (kitchen paper)
Mixing bowls in different sizes
Heatproof glass bowls
Microwave-safe bowls
Saucepans
Wooden spoon

Measuring pitcher (jug)
Weighing scales and measuring cups
Measuring spoons
Wire whisk
Spatula
Pastry brush
Rolling pin
6- or 12-hole muffin pans
12-hole mini muffin pan
Paper muffin or cupcake cups
Baking sheets
Cake pans
Wire cooling rack
Cookie cutters
Baking beans

Baking tips and techniques

Using an oven

- The first thing you need to do for most of the baking recipes is turn on the oven. This is because the oven needs to be hot enough to cook the food you put into it and it takes a little while to heat up.
- The recipe instructions always tell you at what temperature to set your oven. Ask an adult to show you how your oven shows you the temperature and how to set the oven to the correct temperature.
- On most ovens there is a light, which goes out when the oven reaches the temperature you have set, and then it is ready to use.
- It is recommended to use the middle shelf of the oven for most baking needs. Make sure that there is space above it for your cakes or bread to rise.
- Always use oven mitts when putting food into the oven or taking it out and put hot dishes onto a heatproof board or trivet so that you don't burn the work surface.

Preparing your pans

After you have switched on the oven, the first thing you need to do in almost every recipe is to prepare your pan. This is an important step to stop the food you are baking from sticking to the pan as it cooks. If it sticks, you won't be able to lift or turn the food out of the pan. To stop it sticking, you can either grease the pan by rubbing all over the inside with a little oil or butter on a paper towel or line the pan with baking parchment or, for some recipes, do both.

Using the stovetop (hob)

Always ask an adult before using the stovetop.

- When using the stovetop, make sure that saucepan handles don't stick out over the front of the stovetop where you could knock them off.
- Don't have the heat too high—it is easy to burn your food.
- Always remember to turn off the heat when you've finished cooking.
- When you take a pan off the stovetop, always put it onto a heatproof board or trivet so that you don't burn the work surface.

Weighing and measuring

Baking is a little like a science experiment and you need to have exact measurements in order for it to work successfully! This means weighing and measuring out the ingredients very carefully. This book uses two different types of measurements. You can follow one method, but don't swap between the two in your recipe. Use either measuring cups or weighing scales for large quantities, and measuring spoons (or normal spoons) for smaller amounts. Check that the ingredients are level with the top of the spoon, unless the instructions tell you otherwise. Use measuring cups or pitchers (jugs) for liquids.

Butter

Many baking recipes use butter and for these, unsalted butter is usually best. For cake recipes that need you to cream the butter with the sugar, it should be nice and soft, so take it out of the fridge in good time. For pastry recipes and other recipes that need you to rub the butter into flour, the butter should be chilled and hard.

Creaming butter and sugar

- Many cake recipes start with creaming butter and sugar, which means beating them together until they are well mixed and become pale and fluffy. This is an important stage because it makes the cakes light in texture.
- Always remember to take the butter out of the fridge at least half an hour before you need it, so it is soft and easy to cream.
- Creaming is much quicker with electric beaters—but always ask an adult to help with using these.

Rubbing in

Many recipes ask you to rub butter into flour. To do this, first cut up the chilled butter into small pieces and add it to the flour. Then, using your fingers, pick up small amounts of butter and flour, and rub them together between your thumb and fingertips. Keep picking up more of the mixture and rubbing it together. In this way, the butter gradually gets mixed into the flour until there are no lumps left and it looks like breadcrumbs.

Tips for rolling out pastry dough

- When you roll out pastry for small tarts, it is easier to roll out 3 or 4 small pieces, one at a time, rather than one big one.
- Use plenty of flour on your work surface to stop the pastry sticking to the surface. Put some on your rolling pin too.
- When you roll pastry, push down and away from you.
- Keep moving the pastry, to make sure it hasn't stuck, and add a little more flour if it does stick.
- Try not to handle the pastry too much—it needs to stay cold and your hands will make it hot!
- Cut circles for tarts as close together as possible, so you fit lots in before you need to gather up the trimmings and roll again.

Making buttermilk substitute

Some recipes ask for buttermilk, but if you don't have this in your fridge you can make your own buttermilk substitute. Put 1 tablespoon of lemon juice in a measuring cup (jug) and add 1 cup (250 ml) of fresh milk. Stir them together and then let the mixture stand for 5 minutes-the milk will curdle, but taste fine.

Folding cake batter

Some recipes ask you to fold in ingredients. Folding is a way of mixing light ingredients into heavier ones without squashing out any air. Use a metal rather than a wooden spoon to cut through the mixture in a gentle figure eight, rather than stirring it round and round as you would with a wooden spoon. Every so often, scrape around the edge of the bowl to make sure all of the ingredients are mixed together.

Proving dough

The yeast in bread dough is alive and needs to grow (prove) in a warm place until the dough has doubled in size. Find the warmest place in your house to put it—in a warm closet, close to a radiator, near a warm oven, on a sunny windowsill, even on a hot water bottle! If the dough is nice and warm, it will take about an hour to prove. It will still prove if it is colder, but will take much longer.

You need to cover your dough with plastic wrap (clingfilm) to stop it drying out as it rises.

Using a microwave

Using a microwave is a quick and easy way to heat and melt ingredients for baking.

Melting chocolate

Put the chopped chocolate in a microwave-safe bowl. Heat on low for 30 seconds, stir, and heat again for another 30 seconds. Keep checking and stirring at regular intervals of 20–30 seconds, and when the chocolate is nearly melted (when there are a few lumps left), remove the bowl from the microwave and stir the melted chocolate until it is smooth. Take care if the bowl is hot and ask an adult to help you take the bowl in and out of the microwave. Take care that the chocolate doesn't overheat.

Microwave safety

- Always use microwave-safe bowls and never put anything metallic in the microwave.
- When heating anything in the microwave, you must take great care to stir the heated ingredient thoroughly before using or eating it—even if it seems lukewarm on the outside, it could be burning hot inside. When you stir melted chocolate or jelly (jam), for example, you will spread the heat evenly and avoid these hot spots. Heat on a medium or low setting for short lengths of time, rather than continuously, and keep checking at regular intervals.
- Timings given in the recipes are general instructions, but as microwave ovens vary, adapt the timings to suit your particular model.

Warming jelly (jam)

Put the jelly in a microwave-safe bowl and heat on medium for 20–30 seconds. Ask an adult to help you take the bowl out of the microwave and stir it gently. You can heat again for a few seconds longer if necessary, but take care that the jelly doesn't overheat—jelly can become burning hot very quickly.

Using knives

Good cooks must learn to use knives properly and you should ask an adult to teach you. If you use it properly, a sharp knife is safer than a blunt one, because it won't slip, but you must hold the food firmly and keep your fingers out if the way. Always use a chopping board and one of the following three techniques:

1

"Bridge"

The "Bridge" cutting technique is used for cutting larger things (for example apples, tomatoes, or onions) into smaller pieces:

- Hold the food by forming a bridge with your thumb on one side of the food and your index finger on the other side. Hold the knife in your other hand with the blade facing down, guide the knife under the bridge, and cut through the food.
- For some soft items, such as tomatoes, it might be easier to puncture the tomato skin with the point of the knife before cutting.

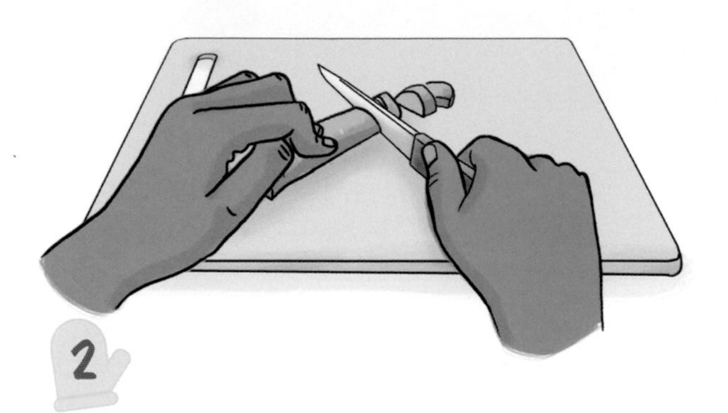

2

"Claw"

The "Claw" cutting technique is used for chopping or slicing foods, such as carrots or onions, into smaller pieces:

- Cut the food in half (using the bridge cutting technique) so that you have a flat side. Place the flat side of the food down on the chopping board so that it is steady.
- Shape the fingers of one hand into a claw shape, tucking the thumb inside the fingers. Rest the claw on the food to be sliced to hold it firm.
- Holding the knife in the other hand, slice the food, making sure to move the "clawed" fingers back as the knife slices closer.

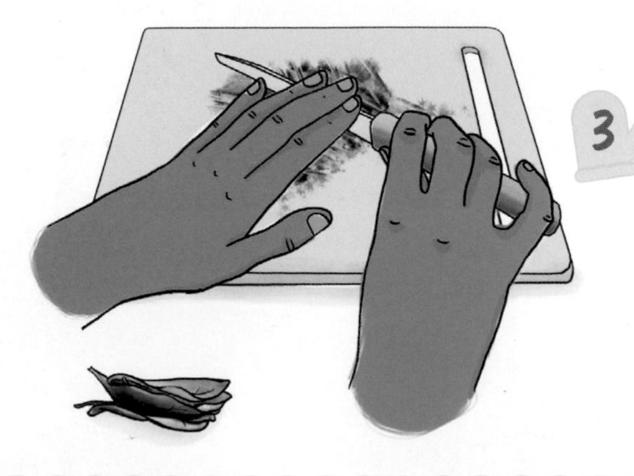

3

Chopping herbs

- Put the pile of herbs on a board. Have the flat of one hand on top of the knife and the other on the handle and rock the knife over the herbs.
- Another way of cutting up herbs is to put them in a small cup and snip them with scissors.

Grating

Cooks grate all sorts of things—cheese, chocolate, carrots, zucchini (courgettes)—to make them small so they will mix into a recipe or be sprinkled on top. Be careful when grating because it is very easy to grate your fingers!

- Stand the grater on a flat chopping board or plate so that it is firm and doesn't wobble. Hold it firmly on the top.
- Hold the food with your fingertips. Grate from top to bottom keeping your fingers well away from the grater.
- Only grate big pieces of food and don't try to grate right to the end—discard the pieces when they get too small to hold safely.

Peeling

To peel carrots (or other vegetables, such as zucchini/courgettes or cucumbers):

- Trim off the ends.
- Hold the carrot at one end and rest the other end on a chopping board.
- Starting halfway along it, run the vegetable peeler down the carrot towards the board and away from your hand.
- Turn the carrot a little and peel the next strip in the same way. Keep turning and peeling until all of one end had been peeled.
- Turn the carrot up the other way, and hold the other end while you peel the second half.

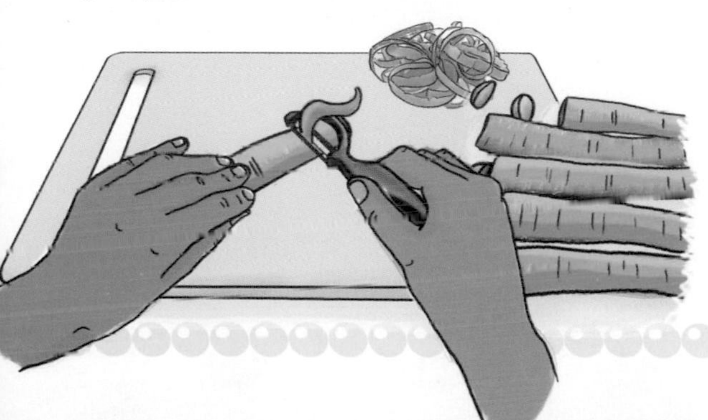

To peel fruit, like apples, or potatoes:

- Rest the apple in the palm of your hand. Starting at the top, run the vegetable peeler around the apple, turning it as you go so that you create a spiral of peel.
- Keep turning the apple as you peel—see how long a strip you can make!

CHAPTER ONE

PERFECT PASTRY

Easy tomato tarts

Puff pastry is such a great ingredient to use. Buy it ready-rolled so that all you have to do is unroll it, cut it into circles, squares, or rectangles, and top with anything you like! This tart is a bit like pizza, but much quicker and easier to make.

You will need

12 oz. (375 g) ready-rolled puff pastry

4 tablespoons sun-dried tomato paste

20 cherry tomatoes

1 ball of mozzarella cheese

a handful of fresh basil leaves

baking sheet

(makes 4 or 6)

1 Ask an adult to turn the oven on to 400ºF (200ºC) Gas 6. Pour a little olive oil onto a piece of paper towel and rub it over the baking sheets to grease them.

2 Sprinkle a little flour over the work surface. Unroll the puff pastry and using a round-bladed knife, cut it into 4 or 6 (depending on how many people are going to eat them) evenly sized squares or rectangles. Lay them onto the baking sheet.

3 Carefully cut all the tomatoes into three slices. To do this hold a tomato with your hand making a bridge (see page 12). Use a sharp knife to cut down onto a board.

4 Use a spoon to spread a little sun-dried tomato paste over the pastry but try to leave the very edges bare.

Arrange the sliced tomatoes over the tomato paste. Arrange them in one layer rather than piling them up.

6

Tear off little pieces of the mozzarella cheese and put them on top of the tomatoes.

Ask an adult to help you put the tarts in the preheated oven and bake for 15 minutes or until the pastry is golden and puffed up and the mozzarella has melted. Ask an adult to help you take the baking sheet out of the oven, and sprinkle fresh basil leaves over the tarts before you serve them.

White chocolate and raspberry tartlets

Like the Easy Tomato Tarts on page 16, these summer tartlets are easy to make because they use store-bought, ready-rolled puff pastry. And they're so pretty!

You will need

10 oz. (300 g) ready-rolled puff pastry

3½ oz. (100 g) white chocolate

2 eggs

½ cup (125 ml) heavy (double) cream

¼ cup (50 g) sugar

2 cups (300 g) raspberries

confectioners' (icing) sugar, for dusting

12-hole muffin pan or tartlet pan

cookie cutter, roughly the same size as the muffin pan holes

(makes 12)

Ask an adult to turn the oven on to 350°F (180°C) Gas 4. Use a little butter on a piece of paper towel to grease the muffin pan holes to stop the tartlets sticking.

2 Sprinkle a little flour over the work surface. Unroll the puff pastry and cut the dough into 12 circles using the cookie cutter. Gently press each circle into a muffin pan hole.

3 Break the chocolate up into small pieces and put it in a small heatproof bowl. Ask an adult to help you set the bowl over a saucepan of gently simmering water, making sure that the bottom of the bowl does not touch the water. Stir the chocolate with a wooden spoon until it has melted. Take it off the heat and let it cool for a while. (You could melt the chocolate in a microwave instead—see page 11.)

4 Break the eggs into a large bowl, pick out any pieces of shell, then beat them with a fork or whisk until they are well mixed and a little frothy.

5

Pour the cream and sugar into the eggs and whisk them all together. Add the melted chocolate and keep whisking until the mixture is nice and smooth.

6

Carefully spoon the mixture into the tartlets until it is just below the top.

7

Ask an adult to help you put the muffin pan in the preheated oven and bake the tartlets for 15 minutes, or until the pastry is puffy and golden and the filling has risen (don't worry, it will sink as the tarts cool). Ask an adult to help you remove the pan from the oven and let it cool.

8

When cool, take the tartlets out of the muffin pan and put them on a cooling rack. Arrange 3 or 4 raspberries on the top of each tartlet. Put a little confectioners' (icing) sugar into a strainer (sieve) and sift it over the tartlets.

Star-topped pies

Topped with a star, these little pies are prettier than plain apple pies, and with the apple mixture spotted with bright red cranberries, they look even prettier when you take a bite, too.

You will need

2 cooking apples

2 red or sweet eating apples

12 oz. (375 g) store-bought sweet pastry

¼ cup (50 g) superfine (caster) sugar, plus extra for sprinkling

½ teaspoon ground cinnamon, plus extra for sprinkling

juice of ½ lemon

⅓ cup (50 g) dried cranberries

1 tablespoon milk

confectioners' (icing) sugar, for dusting

12-hole tartlet pan

fluted round cookie cutter, just bigger than the tartlet pan holes

star-shaped cookie cutter

(makes 9–12)

1 First, prepare the apples. Use a potato peeler to peel the skin from both types of apples. Next, use a sharp knife to cut the apples into halves, then quarters. Remember to cut down onto a board and hold the apple with your hand in a bridge shape (see page 12). Ask an adult to help you carefully remove the cores by cutting a V shape into the center of each quarter. Finally, cut the apples into small pieces (see page 12).

How long a piece of APPLE PEEL can you peel?

2 Tip the apples into a medium-sized saucepan and add the sugar, cinnamon, lemon juice, and cranberries. Ask an adult to help you put the pan over a low-medium heat. Stir the mixture from time to time until the apples are soft.

3 Ask an adult to help you remove the pan from the heat. Let it cool a little and then taste the mixture—add a little more sugar if you want it sweeter. Set it aside until it is cold.

4 Ask an adult to turn the oven on to 350°F (180°C) Gas 4.

5 Use a little butter on a piece of paper towel to grease the tartlet holes in the pan. Sprinkle a little flour on a clean work surface. Roll out the pastry until it is about ⅛ in. (3 mm) thick (quite thin). Use the fluted cookie cutter to stamp out 9 circles. Gently press the pastry circles into the pan holes.

6 Use a teaspoon to put the apple mixture into the pastry cases, filling them almost to the top.

7 Gather up all the scraps of pastry dough, knead them very lightly to bring them together into a ball, and roll the dough out again. Use the star-shaped cutter to stamp out 9 stars for the pie tops.

8 If there is any dough left, gather it together and roll it out again. Make more pairs of circles and stars for more pies.

9 Pour a little milk into a cup. Using a pastry brush, lightly brush the edges of each pie with the milk and top with a pastry star. Press the stars down lightly at the edges to help them stick to the bases. Brush the top of each star with milk.

10 In a small bowl, mix together two tablespoons of sugar with a pinch of ground cinnamon. Sprinkle this over the pies.

11 Ask an adult to help you put the pan on the middle shelf of the preheated oven. Bake for about 25 minutes, or until the pastry is golden brown and the fruit filling is bubbling.

12 Ask an adult to help you remove the pan from the oven. Let the pies cool, then put a little confectioners' (icing) sugar in a strainer (sieve) and sift it over the pies.

Tomato and herb tartlets with feta

Are you or your parents having a party? These sophisticated little tartlets look stunning, taste great, and will impress your friends. Why not have a go?

You will need

12 oz. (375 g) store-bought shortcrust pastry

1 egg, beaten (see page 18)

For the slow-roasted tomatoes:

12 large, ripe cherry tomatoes

4 tablespoons olive oil

1 tablespoon dried oregano

For the herby cheese filling:

1 US extra-large (UK large) egg

⅓ cup (80 g) full-fat cream cheese with garlic and herbs

⅔ cup (150 ml) heavy (double) cream

3 oz. (75 g) feta cheese

salt and freshly ground black pepper

a few fresh herbs such as parsley, basil, or chives (optional)

tiny sprigs of fresh thyme

plain cookie cutter, 2½ in. (6 cm) diameter

2 mini 12-hole muffin pans

foil or baking parchment and baking beans

baking sheet

(makes 24)

1 Put a little butter on a piece of paper towel and grease the holes in the muffin pans. To make the pastry cases, sprinkle some flour onto the work surface and roll out the pastry until it is very thin, about ⅛ in. (3 mm) thick.

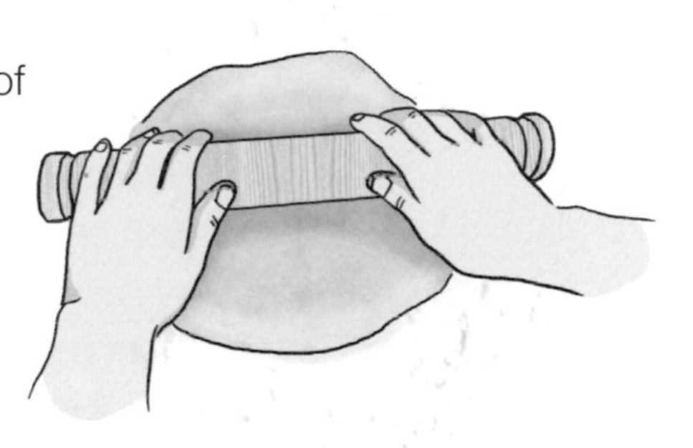

2 Use the cookie cutter to stamp out 24 circles, cutting them close together. You may have to gather the trimmings together and roll them out again.

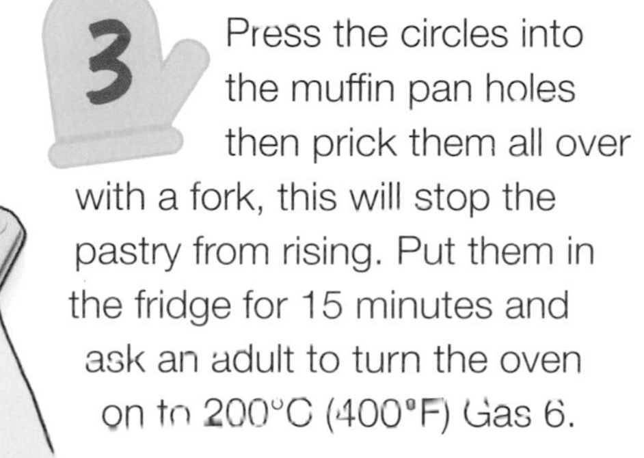

3 Press the circles into the muffin pan holes then prick them all over with a fork, this will stop the pastry from rising. Put them in the fridge for 15 minutes and ask an adult to turn the oven on to 200°C (400°F) Gas 6.

4 To bake blind, put a small cupcake case, or a piece of foil or baking parchment, in each tartlet and fill with baking beans. Ask an adult to help you put the pans in the preheated oven for 8–10 minutes.

5 Ask an adult to remove the muffin pans from the oven and remove the foil or parchment and beans. Return the pans to the oven to bake for 5–7 minutes longer. Now ask an adult to help you brush some beaten egg onto the baked pastry cases and return them to the oven for 5 more minutes until the egg is set and shiny. This will stop the pastry going soggy when you add the filling.

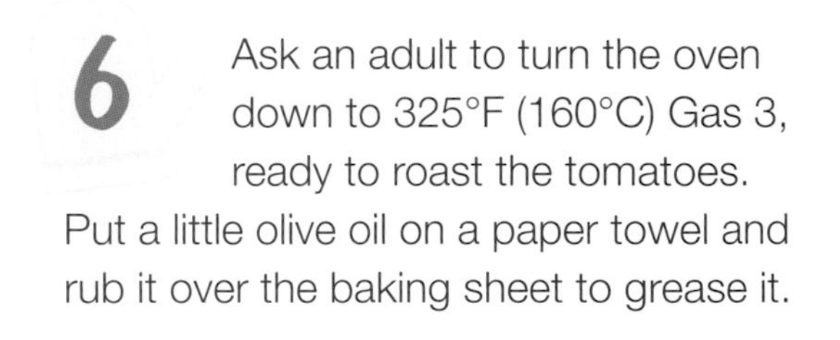

6 Ask an adult to turn the oven down to 325°F (160°C) Gas 3, ready to roast the tomatoes. Put a little olive oil on a paper towel and rub it over the baking sheet to grease it.

7 Carefully cut all the tomatoes in half. To do this, hold a tomato with your hand making a bridge (see page 12). Use a sharp knife and cut down onto a board. Arrange the tomatoes with the cut side up on the baking sheet.

8 Pour the olive oil into a small bowl and add the oregano, a little salt, and lots of ground pepper. Mix it up well and then brush the oil over the cut tomatoes. Ask an adult to put them in the oven and bake them for about 1½–2 hours, checking them every now and then. They should shrivel a bit, but stay bright red—if they get too dark they will be bitter.

CHEESY TARTS with hats on!

9 Now make the cheese filling. First break the egg into a bowl and pick out any bits of shell. Add the cream cheese, the cream, and a little salt and pepper, and beat them together until they are smooth. If you want your tarts to be even herbier, chop the fresh herbs into tiny pieces using a sharp knife and cutting down onto a board (see page 12). Stir them into the cheesy mixture.

10 Cut the feta into 24 small cubes that will fit inside the pastry cases.

11 When it is time for the party, ask an adult to turn the oven on to 350ºF (180°C) Gas 4. Arrange the pastry cases on a baking sheet, put a spoonful of herby cheese mixture in each one and top with a cube of feta. Ask an adult to help you put them in the oven and bake for about 15–20 minutes or until the filling is set.

12 Ask an adult to take the tartlets out of the oven and arrange them on a plate. Top each tartlet with a tomato half. Poke a tiny sprig of thyme into the top of each tomato. Pass them around the party while they are still warm.

Little strawberry tarts

What could be nicer on a summer's day than strawberry tarts? These look really professional with their special shiny glaze. They are best eaten on the day you make them—but who could wait anyway?

You will need

1 lb (450 g) store-bought sweet pastry

2 pints (500 g) small fresh strawberries

about ⅔ cup (225 g) raspberry jelly (jam)

2 baking sheets

(makes 4)

1 Put a little butter on a paper towel and rub it all over the baking sheets to grease them.

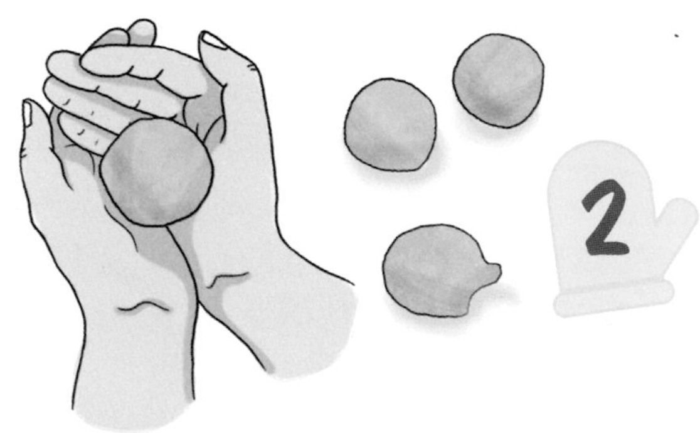

2 Divide the pastry dough into 4 equal pieces and roll each piece of dough into a ball with your hands.

3 Put two pastry balls on each baking sheet, setting them well apart (they will spread in the oven). With your fingers, press and pat out the dough to make circles about ¼ in. (5 mm) thick and about 4 in. (10 cm) across.

4 Pinch the edges of each circle with your fingertips to make a pretty shape, then prick the tart bases all over with a fork (the tiny air holes will stop the base bubbling up in the oven). Chill in the refrigerator for 10 minutes.

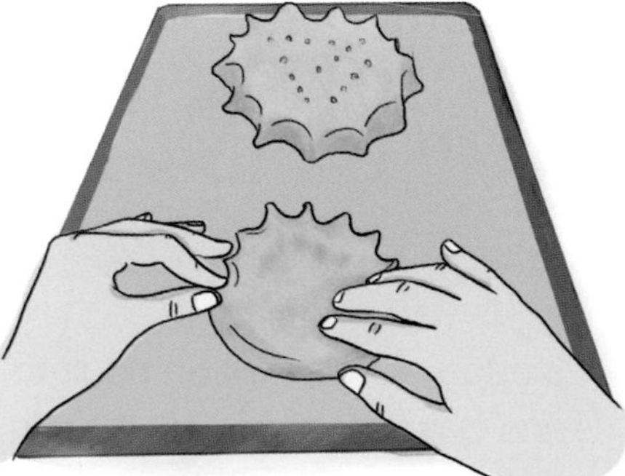

5 Ask an adult to turn the oven on to 350°F (180°C) Gas 4. When the dough is chilled, ask an adult to help you put the baking sheets in the preheated oven and bake for 20 minutes until the tart bases are a light golden color. Carefully remove the sheets from the oven and let the bases cool on the sheets.

Why not make these beautiful tarts as a special treat for someone's birthday party?

Check over the strawberries and throw out any bad ones. Rinse them in a colander and pat them dry with paper towels. Remove the green stems, leaves, and hulls with your fingers or with a small knife.

7

To make the shiny glaze, spoon the jelly (jam) into a small saucepan. Add 1 tablespoon of water and ask an adult to help you heat it very gently, stirring with a wooden spoon. The solid jelly will melt and become a thick, smooth, hot syrup. Remove from the heat before it starts to boil. (You could also heat the jelly in the microwave, see page 11.)

8

Put each of the baked tart bases on a serving plate. Using a pastry brush, brush a little hot glaze over the middle of each circle leaving the edges bare.

9

Arrange the strawberries on top of the glaze with their pointy ends up. Brush the berries with the rest of the hot glaze so that they are completely covered. If the glaze starts to set before you've finished, gently warm it again.

Leave the tartlets until the jelly has set (about 20 minutes) before serving. These are best eaten straight away!

Cheese straws

Cheese straws are delicious nibbles either plain or dunked into dips. They are very quick and easy to make with a food processor, if an adult is helping, but you can make them by hand, too. You can either make giant ones or little finger-sized ones.

You will need

1 cup (125 g) whole-wheat (wholemeal) flour

½ stick (65 g) unsalted butter, softened, plus extra for greasing

3 oz. (85 g) Parmesan cheese

1 egg

baking sheet

(makes 20 small straws or 10 giant straws)

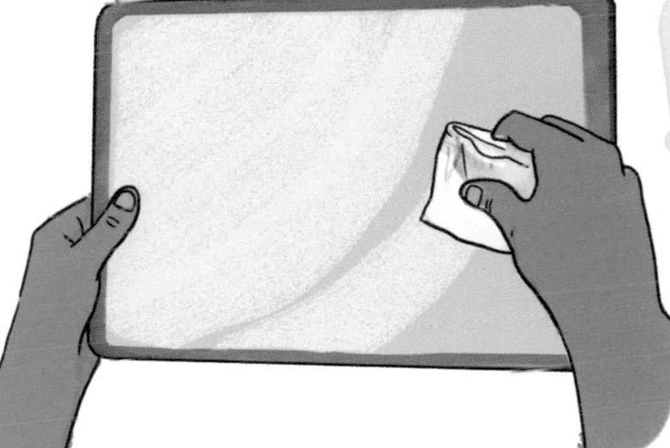

1 Rub the baking sheet with a little soft butter on a paper towel to grease it.

2 Separate the egg yolk from the white. To do this, break the egg onto a small plate, keeping the yolk whole. Now put an egg cup over the yolk and, holding the plate over a bowl, tip the plate so that the egg white slides off. (You don't need the white for this recipe.)

3 If your Parmesan needs grating (you can buy it ready grated), carefully grate it onto a plate using the finest holes on your cheese grater.

GREAT FOR DIPPING!

4 There are two ways to do the next step. If an adult is helping you: blend the flour and butter in a food processor until the mixture looks like fine crumbs. Add two-thirds (2 oz./50 g) of the cheese, the egg yolk, and 2–3 tablespoons water, and process in bursts until the mixture forms a ball.

If you are making the cheese straws by hand: rub the butter into the flour, using your fingers and thumbs (see page 9). Add two-thirds (2 oz./50 g) of the cheese, the egg yolk, and 2–3 tablespoons water. Stir it until the mixture comes together to form a ball. You may find it easier to do this with your hands.

Carefully take the dough out of the food processor or bowl, flatten it slightly, wrap it in plastic wrap (clingfilm), and chill in the refrigerator for 30 minutes.

Ask an adult to help you turn the oven on to 400°F (200°C) Gas 6.

7 If you want long straws, lightly sprinkle your work surface with flour and roll the dough out to about ½-in. (1-cm) thickness, making it into a long rectangle the same width as you want your straws to be. Now cut the rectangle into strips about ½ in. (1 cm) wide. Lay the strips on the baking sheet and sprinkle them with the remaining cheese. For short straws, cut the rectangle in half before you cut them.

8 Lay the strips on the baking sheet and sprinkle them with the rest of the grated cheese. Ask an adult to help you put the baking sheet into the preheated oven and bake for 10 minutes or until the straws are golden.

9 Ask an adult to take them out of the oven. Leave on the tray for a couple of minutes, then transfer to a wire rack to cool completely.

Apple strudel

This recipe uses phyllo (filo) pastry, which is very thin, flaky, and tasty. It comes ready rolled, so it's easy to use, but it looks very impressive. Use sharp apples for this recipe rather than ones that are sweet, but don't have much flavor.

You will need

8 oz. (225 g) ready-rolled phyllo (filo) pastry

9 amaretti cookies

4 medium apples

a generous ⅓ cup (65 g) sugar

1½ teaspoons ground cinnamon

½ stick (60 g) unsalted butter, plus extra for greasing

2 tablespoons slivered (flaked) almonds or raisins, or dried blueberries

confectioners' (icing) sugar, for dusting

cream or yogurt, to serve

large baking sheet

(serves 6)

1 Ask an adult to help you turn the oven on to 400°F (200°C) Gas 6. Rub the baking sheet with a little soft butter on a paper towel. If the phyllo (filo) dough is frozen, let it defrost before you use it. Do not unwrap the dough until you are ready to use it, because it will dry out and become crumbly.

2 Put the amaretti cookies in a plastic bag and tap them with a rolling pin until they have turned to crumbs inside the bag.

3 Now prepare the apples. First, use a potato peeler to peel them all.

4 Use a sharp knife to cut the apples into halves, then quarters. Remember to cut down onto a board and hold the apple with your hand in a bridge shape (see page 12). Ask an adult to help you carefully remove the cores by cutting a V shape into the center of each quarter. Finally, cut the apples into small pieces (see page 12).

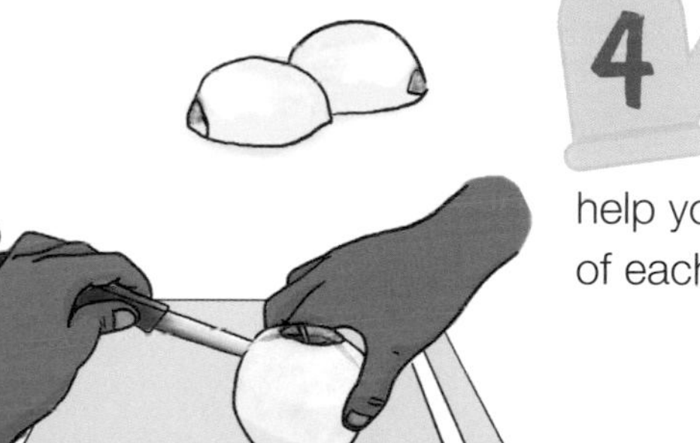

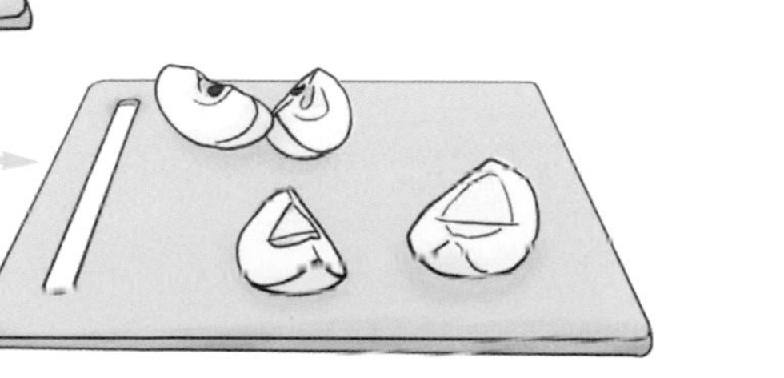

Mix the sugar and cinnamon together in a separate small bowl.

6

Ask an adult to help you melt the butter. Either put it in a small saucepan over the lowest possible heat, or put it in a microwave-proof dish and microwave on medium for about 25 seconds.

7

Unwrap the dough and separate the sheets. Put a large piece of baking parchment on the work surface and then lay the pastry sheets on top, overlapping the sheets to make a rectangle about 22 x 28 in. (56 x 71 cm), with a long side toward you. You need about 4–5 sheets.

Using a pastry brush, lightly brush about half the melted butter all over the dough.

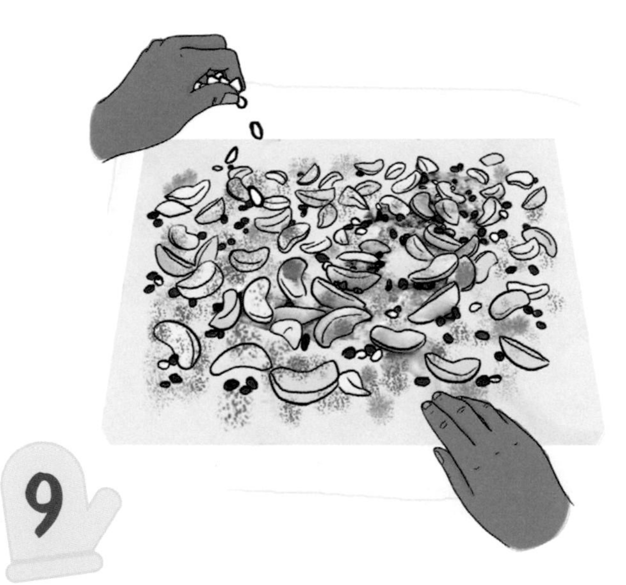

Leaving a clear border of about 2 in. (5 cm) all around the edges, sprinkle the amaretti crumbs onto the pastry, then cover them with the pieces of apple. Sprinkle with the sugar and cinnamon mixture and then add the almonds or dried fruit.

10 Now the really fun part—rolling up the strudel! First, fold over the pastry borders along the two short sides then fold over the pastry border along the long side closest to you. Begin to roll up the strudel from this side, using the baking parchment to help you—but be careful not to roll the paper into the strudel. Don't worry if the pastry splits and the filling falls out, just push it all back together with your hands. Keep rolling until you have a long, thick sausage shape.

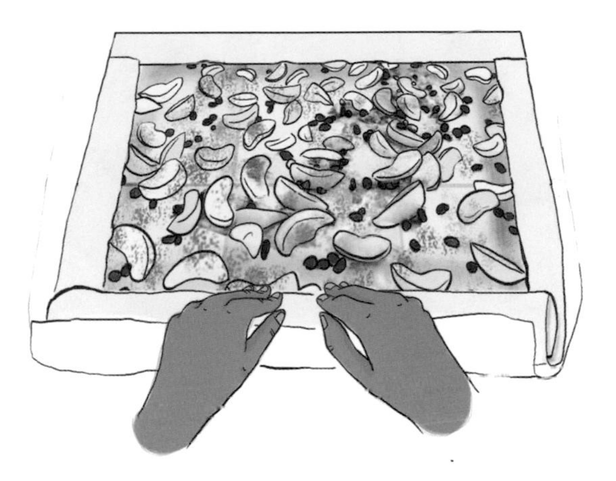

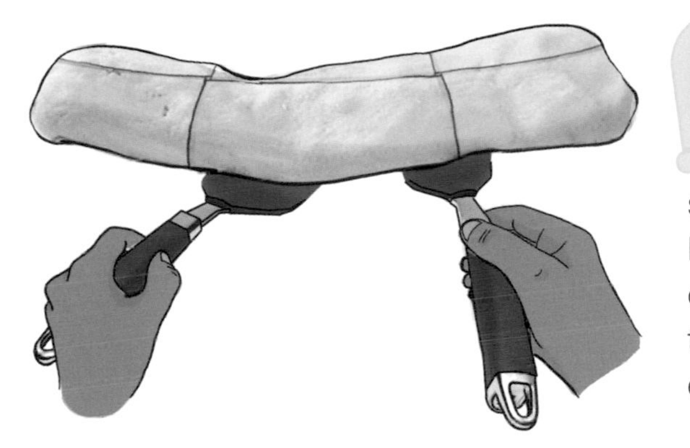

11 It will be difficult to lift the strudel on your own, so ask someone to help you transfer the roll to the buttered baking sheet—use a couple of spatulas to support it. You can lift it in its parchment to help if necessary. If the roll is too big for the size of your tray, you may have to curve the roll into a horseshoe shape. If it splits, press it back together again—it won't show when it's baked! Brush it all over with the rest of the melted butter.

Ask an adult to help you put the strudel into the preheated oven. Bake it for 35 minutes, or until golden brown.

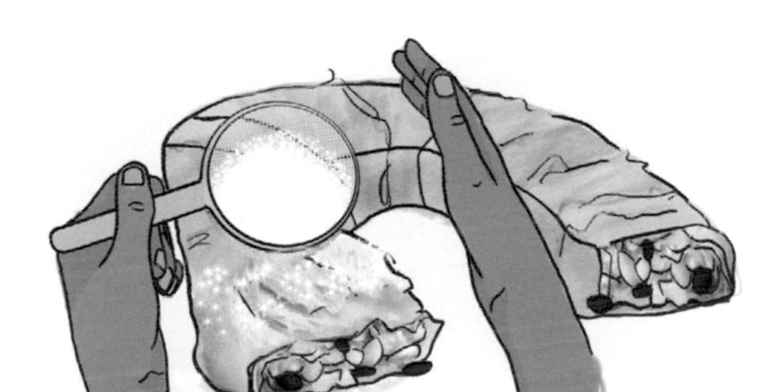

13 Ask an adult to help you remove the baking sheet from the oven, then put 2 tablespoons of confectioners' (icing) sugar into a small strainer (sieve) and sift it over the strudel. Cut it into thick slices and eat warm or at room temperature with cream or yogurt.

CRUNCHY, CRISPY apple strudel!

Toffee-apple tarts

These unusual little tarts are made with real toffees and they are a hit with everyone who makes (and eats) them. It's good to learn how to make pastry and we have given you the recipe here, but you can always cheat and use store-bought sweet pastry instead. And you don't even need to peel the apples!

You will need

For the sweet pastry:

1 stick (125 g) unsalted butter, chilled

1¾ cups (225 g) all-purpose (plain) flour

1 teaspoon sugar

1 egg

1–2 tablespoons cold water

For the filling:

about 6–8 eating apples

12 hard toffee candies

2 x 12-hole muffin pans

3 in. (7.5 cm) round cookie cutter

(makes 24)

1 To make the dough, tip the flour into a mixing bowl. Cut the butter into very small pieces with a round-bladed knife and then rub it into the flour, using your fingers and thumbs, until the mixture looks like fine crumbs (see page 9).

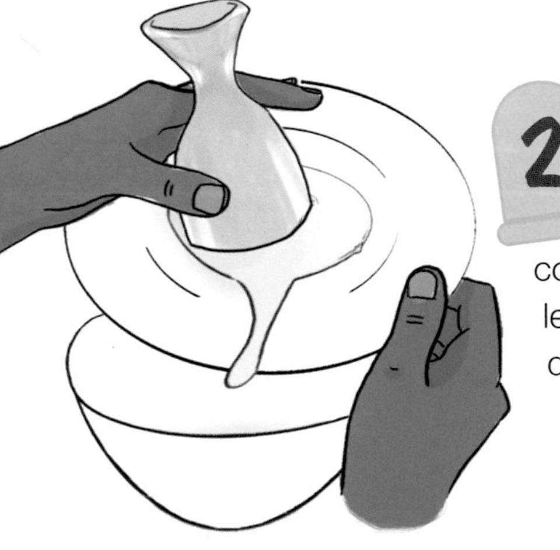

2 Separate the egg yolk from the white. To do this, carefully break the egg onto a plate, cover the yolk with an egg cup, and let the white slide off into a bowl. You do not need the white for this recipe.

3 Add the sugar, egg yolk, and water to the crumb mixture and stir with a round-bladed knife until the mixture comes together and you can form a ball with your hands. Wrap the dough in plastic wrap (clingfilm) and put it in the fridge for 30 minutes—this will make it easier to roll out.

4 Ask an adult to help you turn the oven on to 350ºF (180ºC) Gas 4. Put a little soft butter on a piece of paper towel and rub it around the inside of the muffin pans to grease them.

As it is easier to roll out smaller pieces of dough, break it into 4 pieces. Sprinkle a little flour on the work surface, then roll out the dough, one piece at a time, to about ¼ in. (5 mm) thick.

Sticky TOFFEE APPLES in a tart!

6 Dip the cookie cutter in flour, then cut out 24 circles from the dough. Gently press the circles into the holes of the pans.

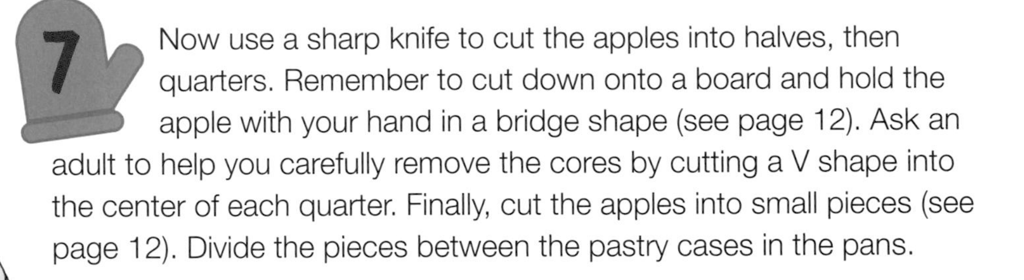

7 Now use a sharp knife to cut the apples into halves, then quarters. Remember to cut down onto a board and hold the apple with your hand in a bridge shape (see page 12). Ask an adult to help you carefully remove the cores by cutting a V shape into the center of each quarter. Finally, cut the apples into small pieces (see page 12). Divide the pieces between the pastry cases in the pans.

8 Put the toffees in a strong plastic bag on a solid work surface and gently bash them with the rolling pin to break them into small pieces.

9 Scatter the broken toffee pieces evenly over the apples, making sure that each tart has a good sprinkling.

10 Ask an adult to help you put the pans in the oven. Bake for 15 minutes until the toffee has melted and the apples are cooked. Ask an adult to help you remove them from the oven. Let them cool for several minutes before taking them out of the pan, because the toffee will be very hot and could burn you.

Mini quiches

You can make the pastry for these yourself if you have the time or, if you want to make them quickly, use store-bought shortcrust pastry instead. You can try all sorts of different fillings—tuna and corn, chopped cooked bacon and cheese, broccoli and salmon. Or be a chef and invent your own filling!

You will need

1 lb (450 g) store-bought shortcrust pastry

1 small onion

1 small garlic clove (optional)

1 tablespoon olive oil

1 egg

⅓ cup (75 ml) heavy (double) cream

⅓ cup (75 ml) milk

2 skinless salmon fillets

Parmesan cheese

2 x 12-hole muffin pans

round cookie cutters to fit your muffin pan

(makes 18)

1 Ask an adult to turn the oven on to 400ºF (200ºC) Gas 6. Put a little butter on a paper towel and rub it around the inside of 18 holes in your muffin pans to grease them.

2 Sprinkle the work surface and your rolling pin with a little flour and roll the dough out to about ⅛ in. (3 mm) thick. Use the cookie cutter to cut out circles, cutting them as close together as possible. When you have cut as many as you can, gather the trimmings together and roll the dough out again. Make about 18 circles.

3 Lay the circles in the muffin pan holes and prick the bottom of each mini-quiche crust once with a fork. This will stop them from rising.

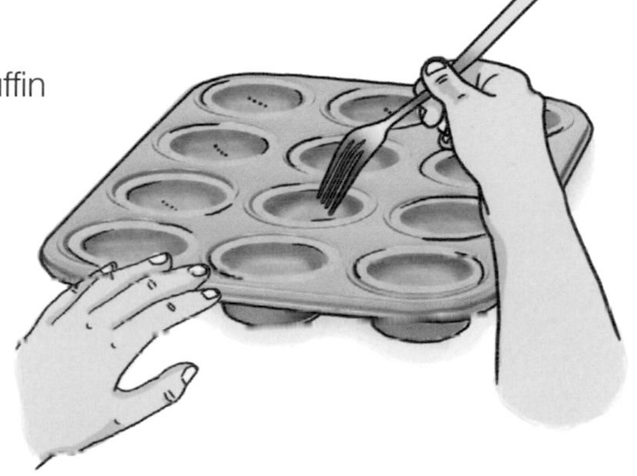

4 Ask an adult to put the pans in the preheated oven to bake for 5 minutes until the crust is a very pale golden color. Remove them from the oven and set them aside (don't take them out of the pan). Leave the oven on.

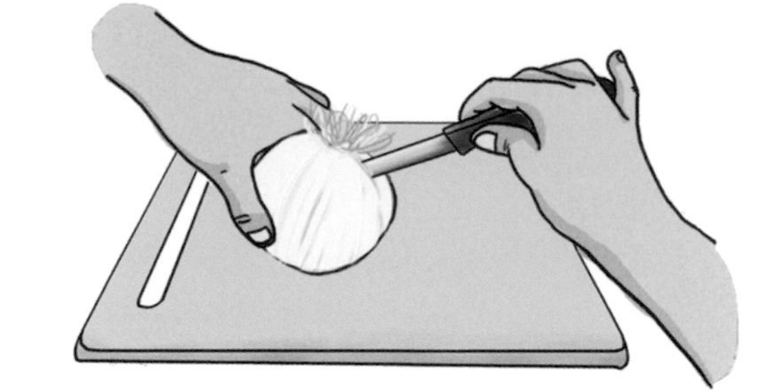

5 Now prepare everything you need for the filling. First the onion: peel off the papery outside skin of the onion and put the onion on a chopping board. Holding your hand in the bridge position (see page 12), cut the onion in half with a sharp knife (be very careful—onions are slippery and the knife can easily slip off). Lay each half flat on the board, trim off any hairy roots, and then cut into very small pieces.

6 If you are using garlic, peel the papery skin off a garlic clove and put the garlic into a garlic crusher, but don't it crush yet.

7 Ask an adult to put a skillet (frying pan) onto the stovetop (hob) on a medium heat. Add one tablespoon of olive oil and when it is hot, add the onion. Crush the garlic straight into the pan. Gently fry the onion and garlic for about 5 minutes, until the onion is soft. Take the pan off the heat and put it to one side to cool a little.

8 Put the salmon on the chopping board and use a sharp knife to cut it into small cubes. Grate the Parmesan cheese onto a plate using a fine grater—you will need a couple of handfuls.

9 Firmly tap the egg shell on the side of a measuring cup and pull the two halves apart with your fingertips. Pick out any pieces of shell. Add the cream and milk, and whisk together using a wire whisk.

10 Now fill the quiches: put a little salmon and a little cooled onion mixture in each pastry case, sharing it out equally. Pour in the egg mixture, until the cases are almost full. Sprinkle each with a little Parmesan cheese.

11 Ask an adult to put the pans into the oven and bake for 5–6 minutes until the quiches have puffed up, the top is slightly golden, and the egg mixture has set firm. Ask an adult to remove them from the oven and let them cool for a few minutes before taking them out of the pan.

PERFECT for a PICNIC!

CHAPTER TWO

SWEET TREATS

Choc-nut granola bars

You can pretend you are making something very healthy when you make these granola bars—there's lots of fruit, nuts, and oats in them—but they are also sweet, buttery, and covered in chocolate chips, making them perfect for a lunchbox treat!

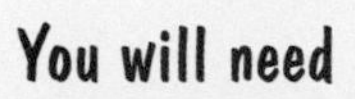

You will need

¼ cup (30 g) whole almonds (optional)

1½ oz. (40 g) milk chocolate

candied (glacé) cherries (optional)

1 stick (125 g) unsalted butter

½ cup (100 g) light brown sugar

4 tablespoons light corn (golden) syrup

2 cups (190 g) rolled oats

½ cup (40 g) shredded (desiccated) unsweetened coconut

9-in (23-cm) square baking pan

baking parchment

(makes 12)

Ask an adult to turn the oven on to 350°F (180°C) Gas 4.

2 Prepare your pan. Put a little butter on a paper towel and rub it all over the inside of the baking pan to grease it. Then place the baking pan onto some baking parchment, draw around it, cut out the square, and fit it into the bottom of the pan.

3 If you are using almonds, carefully cut them into large chunks. Remember to use a sharp knife to cut down onto a board. Put them in a small bowl to use later. Now chop the chocolate into chunks and put that in a different bowl. If you are using them, cut the candied (glacé) cherries into small pieces and set aside.

Chocolate, oats, AND MORE!

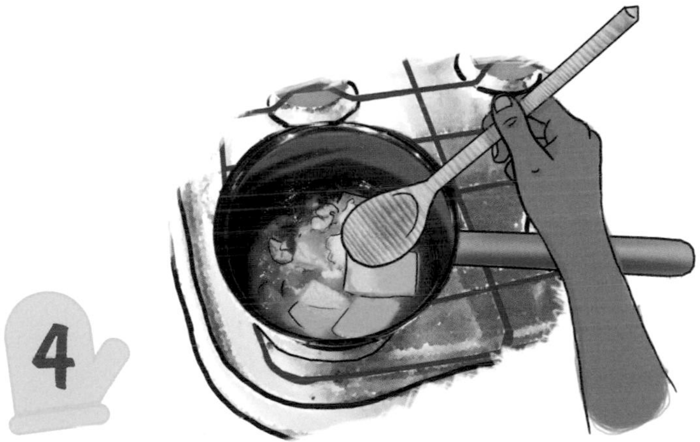

Put the butter, sugar, and corn (golden) syrup into a pan and ask an adult to help you place it on the stovetop (hob) over low heat and stir it until the butter has melted and the sugar has dissolved.

Wipe a little oil over your spoon before dipping it in the corn syrup–the syrup should slide off easily!

Remove the pan from the heat and stir the oats and coconut into the melted mixture.

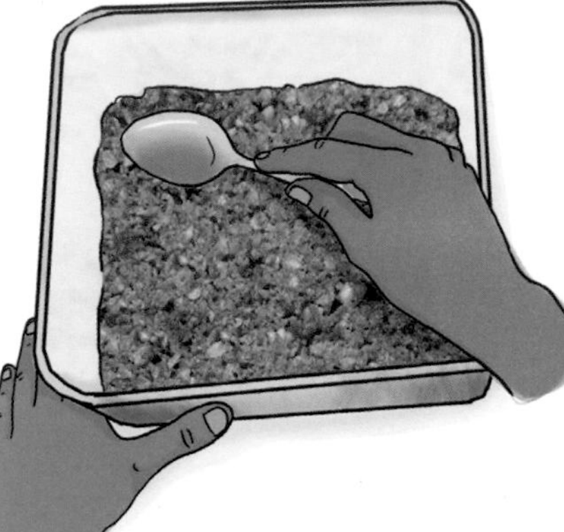

6

Mix everything well, then spoon the oat mixture into the cake pan. Spread the mixture out and press it down evenly with the back of a spoon.

7

Scatter over the almonds and cherries (if you are using them), and press them lightly into the mixture with the back of a spoon.

Ask an adult to help you put the pan into the preheated oven and bake for 15–20 minutes. Ask an adult to remove the pan from the oven and immediately sprinkle over the roughly chopped chocolate so that it will melt a little with the heat of the granola.

9

Mark the granola into bars or squares with a round-bladed knife while it is still warm, then let it cool before cutting through and removing the bars from the pan. These bars will last for 4 or 5 days in a sealed container.

Juicy fruit crisp

A meal always becomes special with a real homemade dessert. You can make your friends or relatives very happy with this one.

You will need

2 large Granny Smith apples or 2 medium pears

1⅔ cups (200 g) fresh or frozen raspberries, blueberries, or blackberries

2 tablespoons white or brown sugar

For the crisp topping:

1 cup (100 g) all-purpose (plain) flour

¾ stick (90 g) unsalted butter

⅓ cup (65 g) brown sugar

medium ovenproof baking dish

(serves 4)

1 Ask an adult to turn the oven on to 375°F (190°C) Gas 5.

2 Put a little butter on a paper towel and rub it all over the inside of the baking dish to grease it.

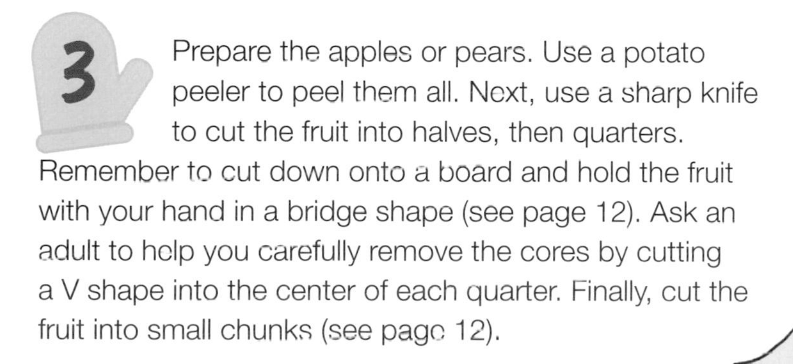

3 Prepare the apples or pears. Use a potato peeler to peel them all. Next, use a sharp knife to cut the fruit into halves, then quarters. Remember to cut down onto a board and hold the fruit with your hand in a bridge shape (see page 12). Ask an adult to help you carefully remove the cores by cutting a V shape into the center of each quarter. Finally, cut the fruit into small chunks (see page 12).

4 Put the fruit in the dish, then add the berries (you don't need to defrost them if they're frozen). Sprinkle with the sugar and toss gently until just mixed. You can use your fingers to do this. Spread the fruit evenly in the dish.

5 To make the crisp topping, chop the butter into cubes and put it in a bowl with the flour. Pick up small amounts of butter and flour and rub them together between your thumbs and fingertips. Keep picking up more of the mixture and rubbing it together. In this way, the butter gradually gets mixed into the flour. When the mixture starts to look like breadcrumbs and there are no lumps of butter, add the sugar and mix it in with your fingers. Squeeze some of the mixture together to make a few lumps.

Scatter the mixture over the fruit in the baking dish —don't press it down. Ask an adult to help you put the dish in the preheated oven and bake for 25 minutes, or until it is bubbling and golden on top.

Ask an adult to help you remove the dish carefully from the oven. You can eat your fruit crisp when it is hot, warm, or cold.

Try this with a scoop of ICE CREAM!

Easter bunny cookies

These cute bunny cookies make wonderful gifts at Easter or can brighten up the tea table at a springtime birthday party. You can buy bunny cookie cutters from bakeware stores or online.

You will need

For the cookie dough:

2 cups (250 g) all-purpose (plain) flour

1¼ cups (140 g) self-rising (self-raising) flour

a pinch of salt

2 sticks (250 g) unsalted butter, at room temperature

⅔ cup (125 g) unrefined superfine (golden caster) sugar

1 egg

1 teaspoon vanilla extract

For the decoration:

1 lb (450 g) white fondant icing

confectioners' (icing) sugar, for dusting

pink and black writing icing

1 yd (1 m) each of blue and pink gingham ribbon

bunny cookie cutters (2 shapes if possible)

2 baking sheets

baking parchment

(makes 12)

1 Set a large strainer (sieve) over a mixing bowl. Pour the two flours and salt into the strainer and then sift them into the mixing bowl. Put the bowl to one side.

2 Put the soft butter and sugar in another large mixing bowl and beat them together with a wooden spoon until the mixture is soft, creamy, and pale. (If an adult is helping, you could use an electric beater.)

3 Carefully break the egg onto a plate and use an egg cup to separate the yolk from the white (see page 29). You do not need the white for this recipe.

4 Add the egg yolk and vanilla extract to the creamed butter mixture and mix all the ingredients together well.

5 Add the flour and stir everything together until all the flour is mixed in and the mixture forms a ball of dough. Stop mixing as soon as the flour is all mixed in.

6 Put the dough in a sealable plastic food bag, or wrap it in plastic wrap (clingfilm), and chill it in the refrigerator for 1–2 hours. When the dough is well chilled, cut some baking parchment to cover your baking sheets and ask an adult to turn the oven on to 400ºF (200ºC) Gas 6.

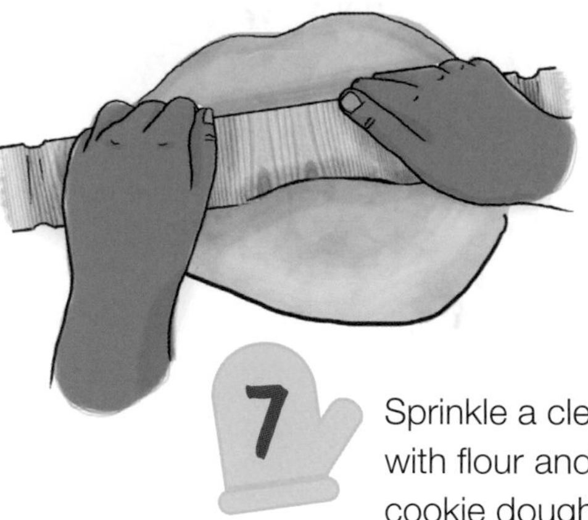

7 Sprinkle a clean work surface with flour and roll out the cookie dough until it is about ¼ in. (5 mm) thick.

8 Use your bunny cutters to cut out as many bunnies as you can, cutting them as close together as possible. When you have cut out the first batch, gather all the trimmings together, roll them out again, and cut out some more.

9 Lay all the cookies on the baking sheets and ask an adult to help you put them into the preheated oven for 12–16 minutes, until the cookies are golden. Ask an adult to take them out of the oven and let them cool on a wire rack.

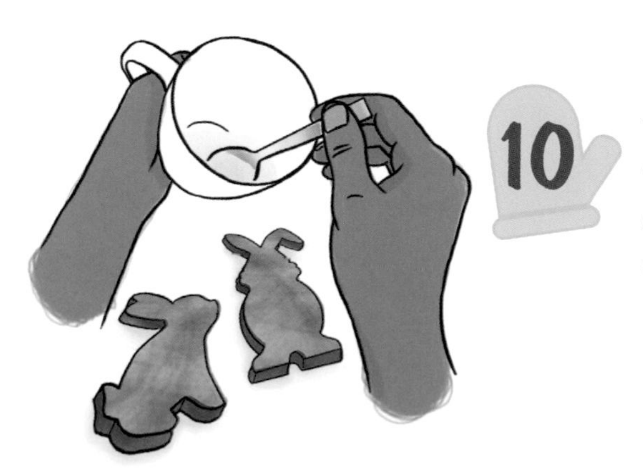

10 To decorate the bunnies, first make a little "edible glue" by putting two tablespoons of sugar in a cup and adding two tablespoons of warm water. Stir them together.

11 Sprinkle a little confectioners' (icing) sugar onto a clean work surface. Roll out the fondant icing until it is about ¼ in. (5 mm) thick. Each time you roll the icing, lift it, turn it a little, and sprinkle on a little more confectioners' sugar to stop it sticking to the work surface. Sprinkle a little confectioners' sugar onto the rolling pin too, if that sticks.

Cute BUNNIES for Easter!

12

Brush a little of your "sugar glue" onto the first cookie. Use the cookie cutter to cut out an icing shape to match the bunny and carefully stick it on. Do the same for the rest of the bunnies.

13

Use writing icing to draw on eyes, noses, tails, and whiskers. To make the fluffy tails, squeeze lots of dots close together. When the writing icing has set, loosely tie a piece of ribbon into a bow around each bunny's neck.

Yummy brownie squares

Scrumptious, deep chocolatey brownies! Top them with a delicious chocolate buttercream frosting and decorate them with colorful candies.

You will need

For the brownies:

⅔ cup (100 g) walnut or pecan pieces

1½ sticks (175 g) unsalted butter

8 oz. (250 g) bittersweet (dark) chocolate

1¼ cups (250 g) superfine (caster) sugar

3 eggs

1 teaspoon vanilla extract

1 cup plus 2 tablespoons (150 g) all-purpose (plain) flour

1 teaspoon baking powder

a pinch of salt

colorful candies and sprinkles

For the chocolate buttercream:

6 oz. (175 g) bittersweet (dark) chocolate

1 stick (125 g) unsalted butter

½ cup (125 ml) milk

1 teaspoon vanilla extract

1¾ cups (225 g) confectioners' (icing) sugar, sifted

9-in (23-cm) square baking pan

baking parchment

baking sheet

(makes 16)

Ask an adult to turn the oven on to 350°F (180°C) Gas 4.

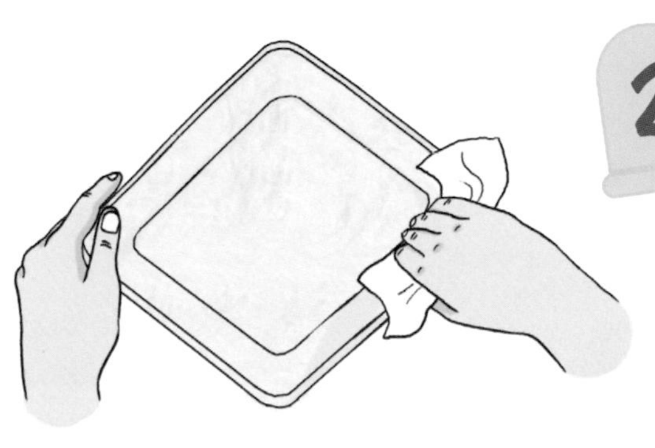

2 Prepare your pan. Put a little butter on a paper towel and rub it all over the inside of the baking dish to grease it. Then place the baking pan onto some baking parchment, draw round it, cut out the square, and fit it into the bottom of the pan.

Spread out the walnuts or pecans on a baking sheet and ask an adult to help you put them in the preheated oven. Toast them for 5 minutes and then ask an adult to help you remove them from the oven. Let them cool.

4 Break or cut the chocolate into small pieces. Cut the butter into small cubes. (Remember always to cut downward onto a board.)

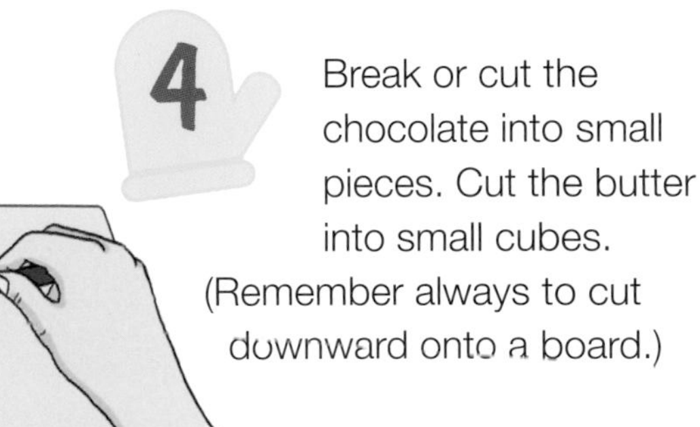

5 Put the chocolate and butter in a heatproof bowl and ask an adult to help you set it over a saucepan of barely simmering water to melt. (You could melt the chocolate in a microwave instead—see page 11.) Stir until the butter and chocolate are smooth and mixed together. Let the mixture cool slightly.

6 Take another bowl and carefully break the eggs into it. Pick out any pieces of shell and then add the sugar and vanilla extract. Use a fork or a wire whisk to whisk them together for 2–3 minutes until they are light and foamy.

7 Using oven mitts (because the chocolate bowl may still be hot), add the melted chocolate mixture to the egg mixture. Stir them together until everything is well mixed.

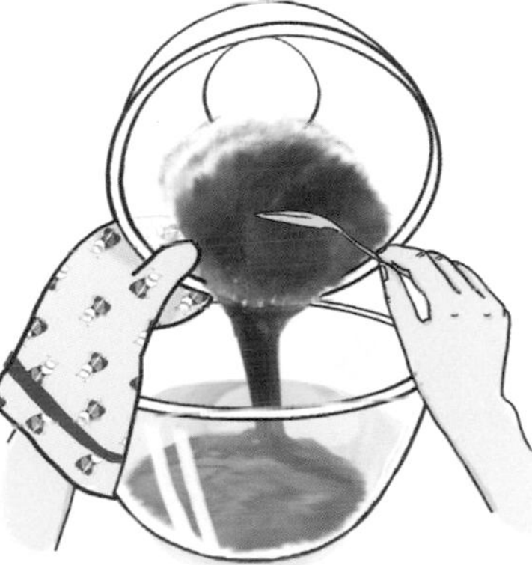

8 Set a strainer (sieve) over the bowl and sift the flour, baking powder, and salt into the mixture. Fold them in using a metal spoon (see page 10) and then stir in the nuts.

9 Pour the batter into the baking pan and spread it out evenly.

10 Ask an adult to help you put the pan on the middle shelf of the preheated oven. Bake for about 30 minutes. Ask an adult to help you remove the pan from the oven. Let it cool.

11 When the brownies are cool, slide a round-bladed knife around the inside edge of the pan to loosen the cake and then turn it out onto a board. Remove the parchment paper from the bottom and turn the cake the right side up.

12 Now make the chocolate buttercream frosting. Just like you did when you were making the brownies, break or cut the chocolate into small pieces and cut the butter into small cubes, and ask an adult to help you to melt them together (see steps 4 and 5 on the previous pages).

13 Put the milk, vanilla, and sugar into a mixing bowl and whisk them until they are smooth. Pour the melted chocolate mixture into the mixing bowl and stir until the mixture is smooth and thick. You may need to leave this somewhere cool for 30 minutes until it is thick enough to spread.

14 Spread the buttercream thickly over the brownies. Decorate with your favorite candies and sprinkles and then cut the brownies into squares.

Little peanut butter cakes

Chocolate and peanut butter go really well together, which makes these little cakes a big hit at any party. Remember to label them clearly so anyone who has an allergy to peanuts can avoid them.

You will need

- 4 tablespoons smooth peanut butter
- 2 tablespoons (30 g) unsalted butter, very soft
- ⅔ cup (125 g) packed soft light brown sugar
- 2 US extra-large (UK large) eggs
- ½ teaspoon vanilla extract
- 1 cup (125 g) all-purpose (plain) flour
- 1 teaspoon baking powder
- 4 tablespoons milk
- ½ cup (100 g) bittersweet (dark) chocolate chips
- confectioners' (icing) sugar, for dusting

12-hole muffin pan
paper muffin cups
heart stencil on page 126
paper

(makes 12)

Ask an adult to turn the oven on to 350°F (180°C) Gas 4. Put a paper muffin cup into each of the holes in the muffin pan.

Put the peanut butter and ordinary butter in a large mixing bowl. Add the sugar and beat with a wooden spoon. (You could ask an adult to help you do this in a food processor instead).

3

Break the eggs into a small bowl. Pick out any pieces of shell, then add the vanilla extract and mix it all up with a fork.

Add a little STENCIL magic!

4

Add a tablespoon of the egg mixture to the butter mixture in the mixing bowl and beat well. Keep adding it, one tablespoon at a time, beating well after each addition, until the egg mixture is all mixed in.

Set a strainer (sieve) over the mixing bowl. Pour the flour and baking powder into the strainer and sift onto the mixture.

Add the milk and then fold everything together with a metal spoon (see page 10). When they are well mixed, add the chocolate chips and fold them in, too.

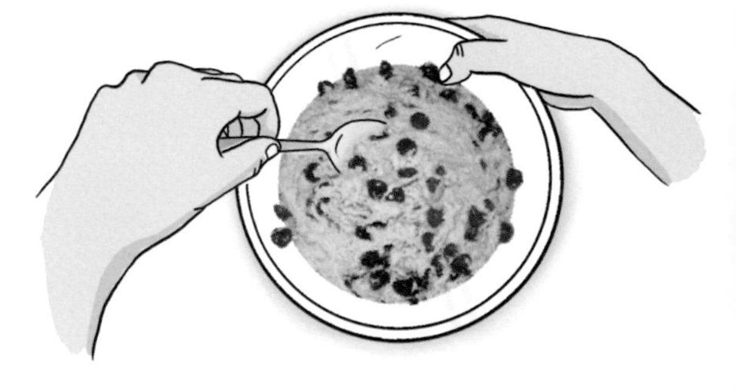

7

Spoon the mixture into the paper muffin cups until they are about one-third full. Ask an adult to help you put the cakes in the preheated oven to bake for 15–20 minutes, until they are a light golden color. Ask an adult to help you remove them from the oven and let them cool on a wire rack.

To stencil a decoration on your cake, trace the heart template on page 126 onto a piece of paper. Using a sharp pair of scissors, make a hole in the center of the heart and then cut out from here around the heart to leave a heart-shaped hole. Hold this stencil on top of each cake and use a pastry brush dipped in milk or water to brush inside the heart where you want the confectioners' (icing) sugar to stick. Be careful not to make it too wet.

Put some confectioners' (icing) sugar in a small strainer (sieve) and sift it over the cakes. Next, shake each cake and the sugar shape will appear. Magic! When completely cold, store your cakes in an airtight container and eat them within 4 days.

Carrot muffins

If you're always being told to eat up your vegetables, these are the cakes for you! You won't even notice the carrots in them because they taste so good.

You will need

8 oz. (250 g) carrots

3 eggs

⅔ cup (125 g) packed soft light brown sugar

7 tablespoons vegetable oil

1 cup plus 2 tablespoons (150 g) self-rising (self-raising) flour

1 teaspoon apple pie spice or a mixture of ground cinnamon and nutmeg

¾ cup (65 g) shredded (desiccated) coconut (if you don't like coconut add more dried fruit instead)

½ cup (75 g) mixed dried fruit, such as raisins, cranberries, and blueberries

12-hole muffin pan

12 paper or silicone muffin cups

(makes about 12)

Ask an adult to help you turn the oven on to 350ºF (180ºC) Gas 4. Put the muffin cups into the holes in the muffin pan.

Use a sharp knife to cut both ends off all the carrots. Remember to cut down onto a chopping board. Now peel the carrots with a potato peeler like this: hold a carrot at one end and rest the other end on the chopping board. Starting halfway down, run the potato peeler down the carrot, away from your body. Be careful—the peeler is sharp! Turn the carrot a little and peel the next strip. Keep turning and peeling until it is peeled all the way around. Now turn the carrot up the other way and hold the other end while you peel the other half.

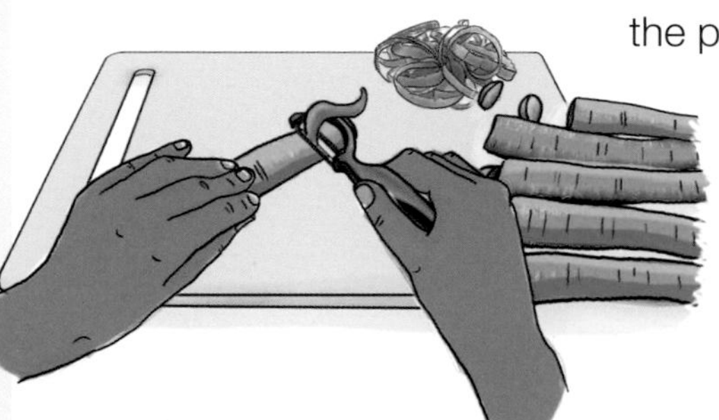

3 Grate the carrots using the smaller holes on the grater—you want the carrots to be grated finely so that they mix into the cake mixture easily.

The BEST WAY TO EAT carrots!

Break the eggs into a large mixing bowl, pick out any pieces of shell, and then beat them with a fork until they are mixed together and a little frothy.

5 Add the sugar to the mixing bowl and whisk together with a wire whisk until the mixture is thick and creamy. (You could ask an adult to help you do this with an electric beater.)

6 Keep whisking and add the oil, a little at a time, until it is all mixed in.

7 Add the flour, apple pie spice (or cinnamon and nutmeg), coconut, dried fruit, and grated carrot to the bowl, and stir with a wooden spoon until everything is mixed in.

8 Spoon the mixture into the paper cups in the muffin pan, so that they are about one third full, putting an equal amount into each one.

9 Ask an adult to help you put the muffin pan in the preheated oven and bake for 12–14 minutes, or until the muffins are baked and golden.

10 Ask an adult to help you take the muffin pan out of the oven and let it cool a little. Then take the muffins out of the pan and put them on a wire rack to cool down until you are ready to eat them.

Raspberry shortbread

This recipe is from Scotland and uses Scottish ingredients—shortcake, raspberries, and rolled oats. It builds up in layers into a heavenly sweet, sticky, crunchy bar.

You will need

For the base:

1½ cups (200 g) all-purpose (plain) flour

¼ cup (25 g) cornstarch (cornflour)

a pinch of salt

⅓ cup (60 g) superfine (caster) or granulated sugar

scant 1½ sticks (150 g) unsalted butter, chilled

For the filling:

1¼ cups (150 g) fresh raspberries

½ cup (125 g) raspberry jelly (jam)

For the topping:

½ cup (40 g) rolled oats (porridge oats)

3 tablespoons light brown muscovado sugar

7-in. (18-cm) square cake pan

(makes 9)

1 Ask an adult to help you turn the oven on to 350°F (180°C) Gas 4. Put a little soft butter on a piece of paper towel and rub it around the inside of the cake pan to grease it.

2 Put the flour, cornstarch (cornflour), salt, and sugar into a mixing bowl and mix together. Cut the butter into very small pieces and rub it into the flour using your fingers and thumbs until the mixture looks like fine crumbs (see page 9). (If an adult is helping, you can do this using a food processor.)

3 Take out one-third of the mixture and put it into another bowl to keep for the topping. Put the rest of the mixture into the greased pan. Spread it out evenly and then press it down with your hand to make a firm, even layer of shortbread. Use your fingers to press it down in the corners and at the edges. If it seems sticky, dip your fingers in a little flour.

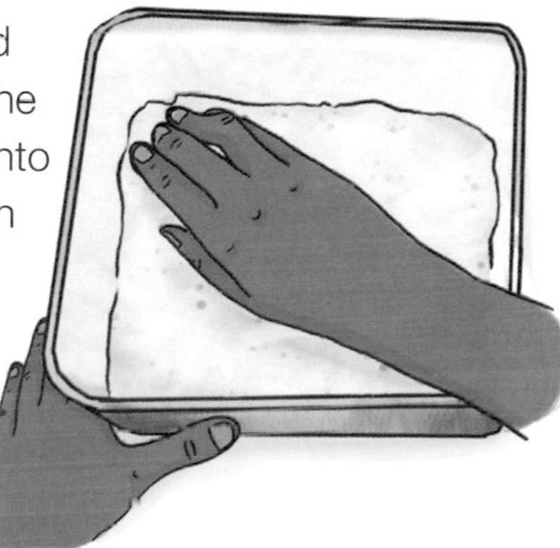

4 Ask an adult to help you put the shortbread base in the preheated oven to bake for 10 minutes, then remove it from the oven. Let it cool while you make the filling and topping. Leave the oven on.

5 Put the fresh raspberries and jelly (jam) into a bowl and mix gently so you don't break up the raspberries. Put to one side.

6 For the topping, put the rest of the shortbread crumbs back into the mixing bowl. Add the oats and brown sugar, mix well with your fingers, and then squeeze the mixture with your hands so it comes together into large crumbs.

7 Gently spread the raspberry mixture over the baked shortbread.

8 Scatter the oat topping evenly over the raspberries.

9 Ask an adult to help you put the pan back into the oven and bake for another 15–20 minutes, until it is a light golden brown and bubbling around the edges. Ask an adult to help you remove the pan from the oven and let it cool on a wire rack.

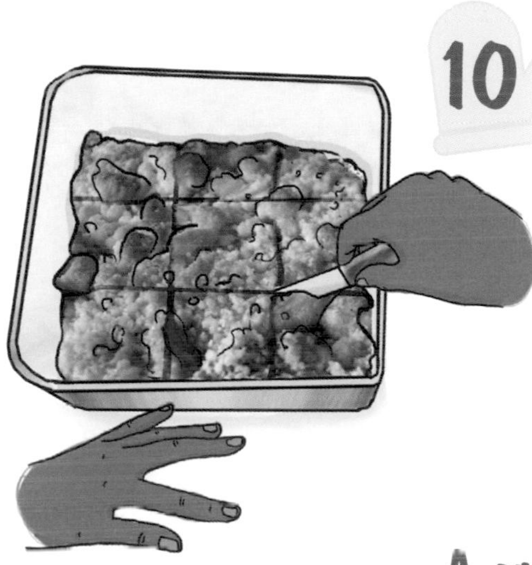

10

When completely cold, run a round-bladed knife around the inside of the pan, then cut the shortbread into 9 squares. Lift each square out with a cake slice. Eat it as a snack or serve with custard as a dessert. You can store your shortbread in an airtight container, but eat it within 4 days.

A crunchy SCOTTISH TREAT!

Chocolate kisses

Who knows where these sweet little chocolate cookies got their name? With a delicious layer of raspberry cream sandwiched between them, little kisses are quick and easy to make and taste scrumptious.

You will need

For the chocolate kisses:

1¾ sticks (200 g) unsalted butter, softened

½ cup (100 g) natural cane sugar or granulated sugar

1 teaspoon vanilla extract

2 cups (250 g) self-rising (self-raising) flour

2 tablespoons cocoa powder

For the raspberry cream:

a few ripe raspberries (about 4–5)

scant stick (100 g) unsalted butter, softened

⅔ cup (100 g) confectioners' (icing) sugar

2 baking sheets

(makes 25)

1 Ask an adult to help you turn the oven on to 350°F (180°C) Gas 4. Put a little butter on a piece of paper towel and rub it all over the baking sheets to grease them.

2 Put the soft butter, sugar, and vanilla extract in a mixing bowl and mix well with a wooden spoon until the mixture becomes fluffy and paler in color.

3 Add the flour and cocoa powder to the bowl and mix well with your hands until it comes together into a dough.

Make chocolate kisses for SOMEONE YOU LOVE!

4 Pull off a small piece of dough and roll it into a ball about the size of a walnut. Then flatten it a little. Put it onto a baking sheet. Roll another one—make sure it is about the same size—and keep going until you have about 50 cookies (make sure you have an even number).

Ask an adult to help you put the baking sheets in the oven. Bake for 6–7 minutes and then ask an adult to help you take the sheets out of the oven. Let them cool.

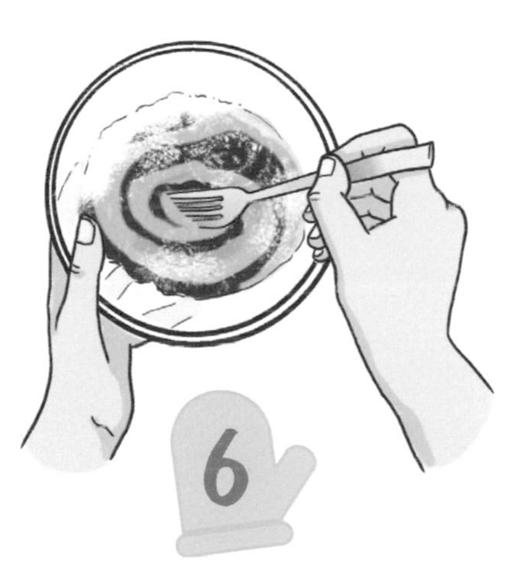

6

For the raspberry cream, put the berries into a small bowl and mash them with a fork. Add the butter and sugar and mix them all together with the fork.

7 Spread a little cream onto a cookie and sandwich it together with another cookie. Keep going until you have 25 kisses.

Baked Alaska

A hot, meringue-topped cake with a freezing ice cream surprise inside—that's what a Baked Alaska is, and what could be more fun to make and eat! For a quicker way to make this, you could use a ready-made sponge cake for the base.

You will need

For the sponge cake:

¾ cup plus 2 tablespoons (115 g) all-purpose (plain) flour

1 teaspoon baking powder

½ cup plus 1 tablespoon (115 g) superfine (caster) sugar

1 stick (125 g) unsalted butter, very soft

½ teaspoon vanilla extract

2 US extra-large (UK large) eggs

1 tablespoon milk

To finish:

1 pint (500 ml) strawberry ice cream (or your favorite flavor)

4 eggs

1 cup plus 2 tablespoons (225 g) superfine (caster) sugar

1½ cups (150 g) raspberries

round cake pan, 8 in. (20 cm) diameter

baking parchment

baking sheet

(makes 1 large cake)

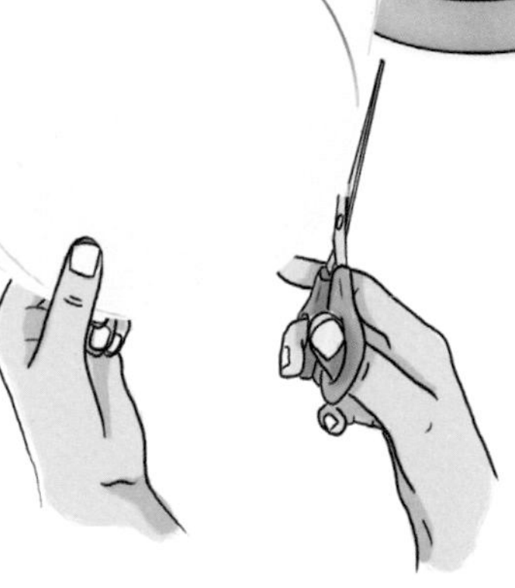

1 Ask an adult to help you turn the oven on to 350°F (180°C) Gas 4. Put the pan on the baking parchment and draw around it. Cut just inside the line to make a disk of paper. Put a little soft butter on a piece of paper towel and rub it around the inside of the cake pan. Fit the parchment disk into the base of the pan and put it to one side.

2 Put a strainer (sieve) over a mixing bowl and sift the flour and baking powder into the bowl. Stir in the sugar, then add the very soft butter and vanilla.

3 Break the eggs into a small bowl. Pick out any pieces of shell, then add the milk and lightly beat them with a fork to break them up. Pour the eggs into the mixing bowl. Beat all the ingredients with a wooden spoon (or ask an adult to help you use an electric hand-held beater), until the mixture is very smooth and light. Spoon the mixture into the prepared cake pan and spread it evenly around the pan.

4

Ask an adult to help you put the sponge cake in the preheated oven to bake for about 25 minutes, until it is a light golden brown. To test if the cake is baked, ask an adult to help you remove it from the oven and gently press it in the middle. If it springs back it is baked; if there is a dimple, then bake for 5 minutes more. Ask an adult to help you remove the sponge from the oven. Leave it for 2 minutes, then run a round-bladed knife around the inside of the pan and carefully turn out the cake onto a wire rack. Leave it to cool completely.

5

When the cake is cold, remove the ice cream from the freezer and leave it until it is soft enough to scoop out easily. Put the sponge cake onto a baking sheet, then scoop or spoon the ice cream on top and spread it out to make an even layer using a palette knife. Put the whole thing back into the freezer and leave it until the ice cream is very firm—at least 1 hour, but you can leave it in the freezer for up to 3 days.

6

When you are ready to finish the Alaska, ask an adult to help you turn the oven on to 425°F (220°C) Gas 7. Then separate the egg whites from the yolks. To do this, carefully break one egg at a time onto a plate, place an egg cup over the yolk, and let the white slide off into a very clean mixing bowl (see page 29). You do not need the yolks for this recipe, so put them into another bowl to use for something else.

7 Stand the bowl on a damp cloth to keep it from wobbling as you whisk the eggs. If you can, ask an adult to help you use an electric beater at this stage, it will be much quicker and easier, but you can whisk by hand. Whisk the egg whites until they turn into a stiff white foam. You'll know if you have whisked enough when you lift out the whisk and there are sharp little peaks of white standing up in the bowl.

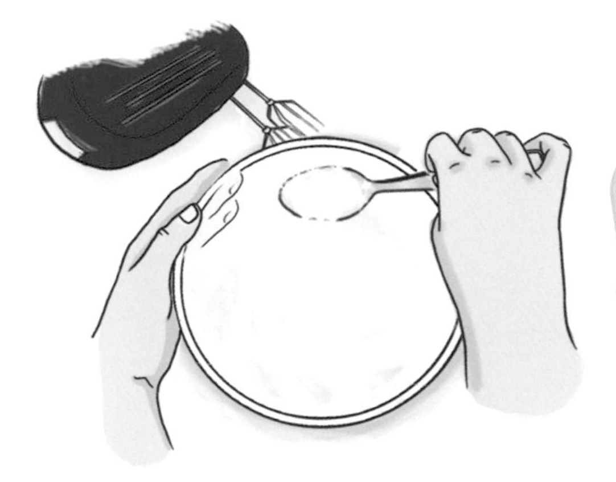

8 Now add 2 tablespoons of the superfine (caster) sugar and whisk it into the egg white, then add two more and whisk again. Keep going until you have whisked in all the sugar and have made a stiff, glossy meringue.

For the next stages you need to work really quickly so that the ice cream doesn't melt. First, check that the oven is really hot then remove the sponge and ice cream from the freezer. Quickly arrange the raspberries on top of the ice cream.

10 Now quickly cover the whole thing with the meringue, spreading it all over the top and sides of the cake, right down to the baking sheet. Make a few peaks in the topping. The meringue stops the ice cream from melting, so there must be no holes or gaps!

11 Ask an adult to help you put the Alaska in the oven to bake for just 4–5 minutes, until it is lightly browned. Any longer and the ice cream will melt. Serve immediately!

Chocolate swirl cake

For this cake, two different flavors and colors are swirled together to make lovely patterns. It is very pretty when you slice it, and you could always add a few drops of food coloring to the vanilla mix to make the colors even more dramatic!

You will need

2 oz. (50 g) bittersweet (dark) chocolate, chopped

1½ cups (175 g) all-purpose (plain) flour

1 rounded teaspoon baking powder

1½ sticks (175 g) unsalted butter, softened

1 cup (200 g) superfine (caster) sugar

4 eggs

2 teaspoons vanilla extract

2 tablespoons milk

1 quantity Chocolate Buttercream (see page 54)

chocolate chips and sprinkles

2-lb. (1-kg) loaf pan, or 2 x 1-lb. (500-g) loaf pans

Makes 1 large or 2 small loaf cakes

1 Ask an adult to turn the oven on to 350°F (180°C) Gas 4. Put a little butter on a piece of paper towel and wipe it around the inside of the pan to grease it. Put the loaf pan on the baking parchment and draw around the base. Take the pan off and make the rectangle longer at both ends so that, when you cut it out, the parchment is long enough to cover the base and stretch up both ends of the pan. Cut it out just inside the line and fit it into the pan (it should stick to the butter).

2 Ask an adult to help you put the chocolate in a heatproof bowl over a pan of barely simmering water, making sure the bottom of the bowl doesn't touch the water. Stir very carefully until melted or melt the chocolate in the microwave (see page 11).

3 Put a strainer (sieve) over a mixing bowl and sift in the flour and baking powder together.

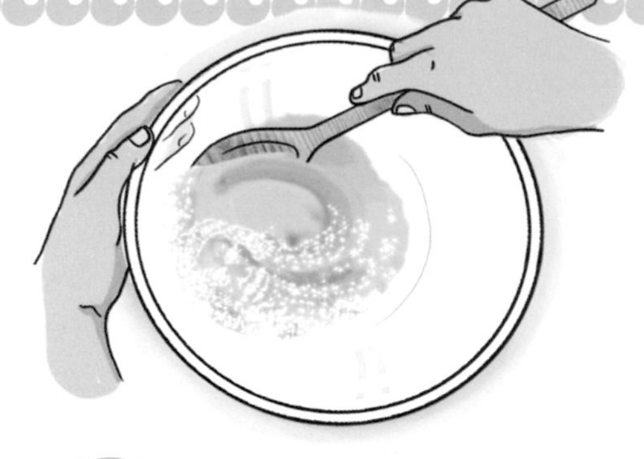

4 Put the butter and sugar in another bowl and beat them together with a wooden spoon until they are pale and fluffy. (If an adult is helping, this is quicker and easier to do with an electric beater.)

Firmly tap each egg on the side of a third bowl and pull the two halves apart with your fingertips. Pick out any pieces of shell. Whisk them up and then gradually add them, a tablespoonful at a time, to the butter and sugar. Each time you add some egg, mix it in really well before you add any more. Scrape down the side of the bowl with a rubber spatula from time to time, especially if you are using an electric beater. Add the vanilla and mix it in.

6 Tip the sifted flour and baking powder into the batter and mix until smooth. Stir in the milk.

7 Spoon half of this mixture into the melted chocolate and mix it in until smooth.

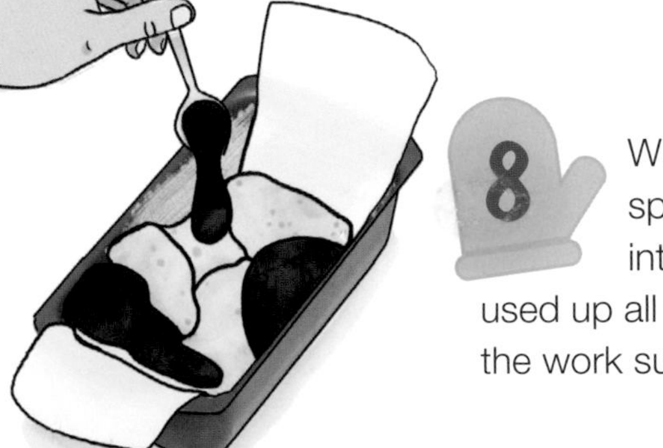

8 With a large spoon, drop alternate spoonfuls of vanilla and chocolate batter into the prepared loaf pan. When you have used up all the batter, give the pan a sharp tap on the work surface to level the mixture.

9

Now the really fun part! To create the swirly, marbled effect, drag the blade of a round-bladed knife through the mixture with a cutting action, going in different directions to create swirls. Don't do this too much or it will all just mix together without the pretty patterns.

10 Ask an adult to help you put the pan on the middle shelf of the preheated oven. Bake for about 40–45 minutes, or until a toothpick pushed into the middle of the cake comes out clean. Ask an adult to help you take the cake out of the oven. Let it cool for 15 minutes. Loosen the sides with a round-bladed knife, then carefully lift it out of the pan, by holding the ends of the paper. Put it onto a wire rack to cool completely.

11 Make some Chocolate Buttercream (see page 54) and spread it all over the top of the cold cake. Decorate it with assorted chocolate chips and sprinkles.

CHAPTER THREE

DELICIOUS DOUGH

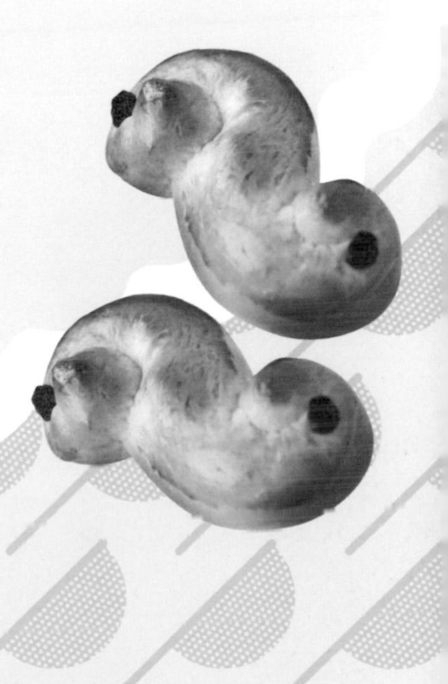

Tomato pesto rolls

It is fun to rub the ingredients together to make the dough for these pretty little rolls, but it is quicker to make them in a food processor. The rolls are best freshly baked and still warm, or you could split them in half and toast them the next day.

You will need

4 cups (500 g) self-rising (self-raising) flour

½ teaspoon salt

1 cup (225 g) natural cottage cheese

a small handful of fresh basil leaves

1 US extra-large (UK large) egg

about ⅔ cup (150 ml) milk

5 cherry tomatoes

2 tablespoons pesto (or olive oil)

baking sheet

baking parchment

(makes 10 small rolls)

1 Ask an adult to turn the oven on to 375°F (190°C) Gas 5. Cut a piece of baking parchment to fit the baking sheet and sprinkle it with a little flour. Put it to one side.

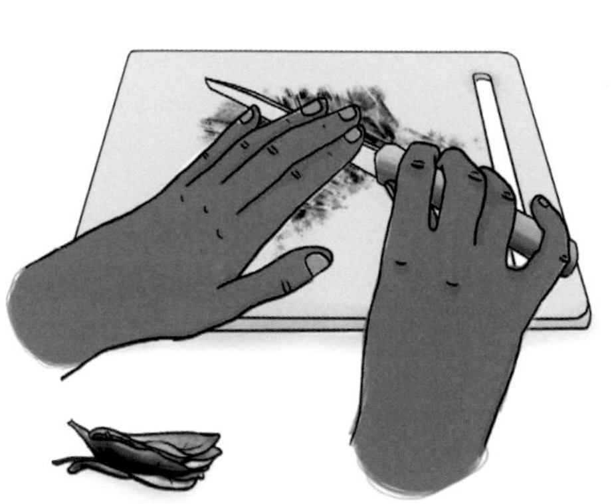

2 Count out ten basil leaves and put them to one side. If you are making the rolls by hand, tear or chop up the rest of the basil leaves, carefully using a sharp knife and remembering to cut down onto a board (see page 12). You won't need to chop the basil if you are using a food processor.

3 Put the flour, salt, cottage cheese, and basil into a mixing bowl and, using your fingers and thumbs (see page 9), rub the cheese into the flour until everything is mixed together and looks like crumbs (or ask an adult to help you do this in a food processor).

4 Break the egg into another bowl, pick out any pieces of shell, then add the milk and beat them together with a fork.

5 Add the egg mixture to the flour and cheese, stir it with a wooden spoon until it is mostly mixed in and then use your hands to gather it all together into a ball. If there are dry crumbs and the dough feels hard and dry, add a splash more milk.

(If you are using a food processor, ask an adult to help you run the machine and pour in the egg/milk mix through the feed tube. Stop the processor when the ingredients have come together to make a ball of soft dough. If there are dry crumbs and the dough feels hard and dry, add a little more milk.)

Will your tomatoes POP out of your rolls?

6

Sprinkle a little flour over the work surface and turn out the dough (ask an adult to help you remove the processor blade if you are using a food processor). Wash your hands if they are sticky, dry them, and then dust a little flour over them. Now gently knead the dough. To do this, push the ball of dough down and away from you with the heel of your hand, stretching and flattening it as you push. Fold the far edge toward you. Turn the ball around half a turn and stretch the dough out again. Fold and turn again. Keep doing this until the dough is silky smooth and stretchy.

7

Divide the dough into 10 equal pieces and roll each piece into a ball. Arrange the balls slightly apart on the baking sheet. Push a deep hole into the center of each one with your finger or thumb.

8

Using a sharp knife, cut the tomatoes in half. Push a basil leaf into each hole in the dough, then a tomato half—cut-side up. Make sure the tomato is deep in the hole in the dough or it will pop out during baking!

9

Use a pastry brush to brush the top of each roll with pesto or olive oil.

10

Ask an adult to help you put the rolls in the preheated oven and bake them for about 20 minutes, until they are golden brown. Ask an adult to help you take the baking sheet out of the oven and put it on a wire rack. Let the rolls cool for at least 10 minutes before you eat them.

Scandinavian buns

These buns are traditionally served on St Lucy's Day, December 13th, in Sweden, where they call them "lussekatter." They are normally made into a backward "S" shape, but you could make them into any shape you like—why not try simple animal shapes with raisins for eyes? Making dough with yeast is always magical because you can watch it rise and fill with bubbles as the yeast begins to work.

You will need

1 cup (250 ml) milk

a good pinch of saffron strands

4–4¾ cups (500–600 g) strong (bread) flour

1 package (¼ oz./7 g) active dry yeast

½ teaspoon salt

¼ cup (50 g) sugar

3 tablespoons (45 g) unsalted butter, softened

⅓ cup (100 ml) sour cream, at room temperature

1 egg

24 raisins

2 baking sheets

baking parchment

(makes 12)

1 Cut pieces of baking parchment to fit the baking sheets.

2 Ask an adult to help you heat the milk in a small saucepan or in the microwave (see page 11), until it is hot but not boiling. Turn off the heat and drop the saffron strands in and let them soak in the hot milk for 10 minutes to flavor it and turn it yellow.

3 Tip 4 cups (500 g) of the flour, the yeast, salt, sugar, butter, and sour cream into a large mixing bowl and stir it all together. Pour in the warm milk and use your hands to mix it into the other ingredients until you get a dough. If the dough feels very dry and hard to mix, add a little more milk. If it is very sticky, add a little more flour.

4 Sprinkle a little flour onto a clean work surface. Shape the dough into a ball, tip it out onto the work surface, and begin to knead it. To do this, push the ball of dough down and away from you with the heel of your hand, stretching and flattening it as you push. Fold the far edge toward you. Turn the ball around half a turn and stretch the dough out again. Fold and turn again. Keep doing this until the dough is silky smooth and stretchy—this will take up to 7 minutes and you may need to add more flour if the dough is too sticky.

5 Shape the dough into a neat ball again. Wash and dry the bowl and put the dough back into it. Cover the bowl tightly with plastic wrap (clingfilm) and put it in a warm place for the dough to rise. It needs to double in size, which will take about an hour or longer if you haven't got anywhere warm to leave it.

6 Tip the dough onto the floured work surface and knead it again for 1 minute. Divide it into 12 equal pieces. Roll each piece into an 8-in. (20-cm) long sausage and twist into a backward "S" shape. Place 6 of the buns on one of the baking sheets and the other 6 on the other sheet.

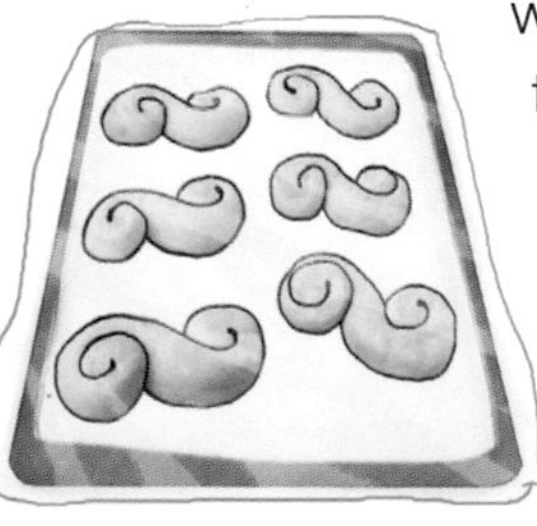

7 Pour a little oil onto a paper towel and use it to wipe over two large pieces of plastic wrap. Use the wrap to cover the baking sheets loosely (oiled-side down). Let the buns rise again for a further 30 minutes in a warm place.

8 About 10 minutes before the buns are ready to be baked, ask an adult to turn the oven on to 375ºF (190ºC) Gas 5.

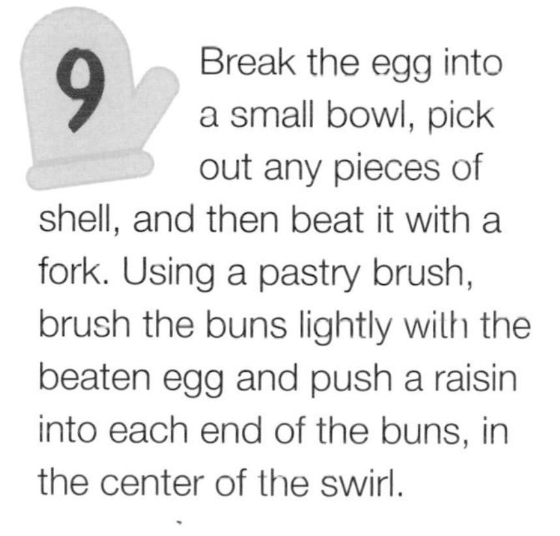

9 Break the egg into a small bowl, pick out any pieces of shell, and then beat it with a fork. Using a pastry brush, brush the buns lightly with the beaten egg and push a raisin into each end of the buns, in the center of the swirl.

10 Ask an adult to help you put the baking sheets on the middle shelf of the preheated oven. Bake for about 12–15 minutes, until well risen, shiny, and deep golden brown.

Mini pizzas

If you've never made pizza, you've been missing out! It's lots of fun because you can make them any size or shape you like and choose all your favorite toppings.

1 Ask an adult to turn the oven on to 400°F (200°C) Gas 6. Pour a little olive oil onto a piece of paper towel and rub it over the baking sheets to stop the pizzas sticking.

To make the pizza bases, set a strainer (sieve) over a large mixing bowl. Tip the flour, sugar, baking soda, and salt into the strainer and sift into the bowl.

You will need

For the pizza bases:

3 cups (400 g) all-purpose (plain) flour

1 teaspoon sugar

1 teaspoon baking soda (bicarbonate of soda)

1 teaspoon salt

½ teaspoon dried oregano

1½ cups (350 ml) buttermilk (see page 10)

For the topping:

14-oz. (400-g) can chopped tomatoes

1 tablespoon tomato paste (purée)

1 tablespoon olive oil

1 teaspoon dried oregano

1 garlic clove

10 oz. (300 g) mozzarella cheese

choice of topping, such as pitted olives, slices of pepperoni or ham, sliced red or green bell pepper, or mushrooms

sea salt and freshly ground black pepper

2 large baking sheets

(makes 4 medium pizzas)

3 Stir in the oregano and then make a hole in the center of the flour and pour in the buttermilk. Using one hand, start to mix the flour into the liquid, then gradually work all the flour into the dough to make a soft and slightly sticky mixture. If there are dry crumbs, and it is hard to work all the flour into the dough, add 1 tablespoon of buttermilk or milk. If the dough is really sticky and feels wet, work in more flour, one tablespoon at a time.

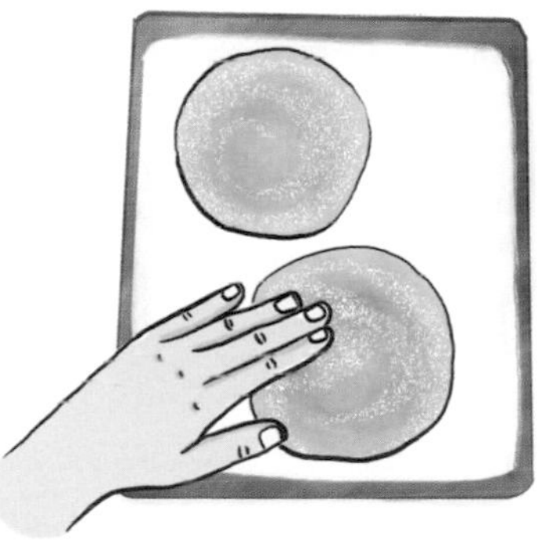

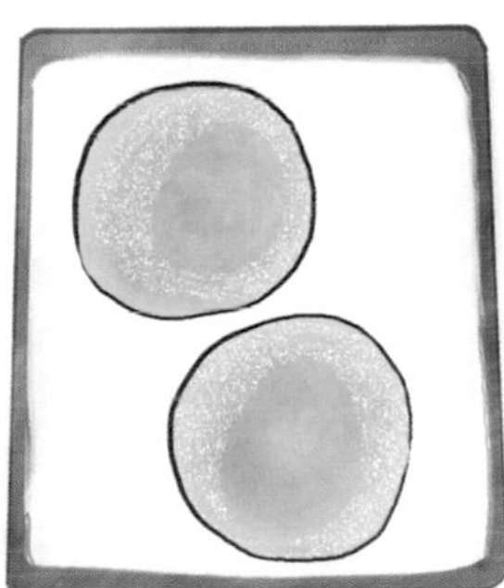

4 Sprinkle a little flour over the work surface. When the dough comes together in a ball, tip it out of the bowl onto the work surface. Knead the ball of dough with both hands by squashing and squeezing it for 1 minute, or until it looks smooth.

5 Divide the dough into 4 equal pieces and shape each piece into a ball. Rub flour onto your hands, then gently pat out each piece of the dough into a circle about 7 in. (13 cm) across. Set the circles slightly apart on the prepared baking sheets.

PERFECT pizzas for a PARTY!

6 To make the pizza topping, set a large strainer (sieve) over a bowl, then tip the can of tomatoes into the strainer and let them drain for a couple of minutes.

7 Ask an adult to help you use a food processor or blender for the next stage. First, peel the garlic clove, then tip the tomatoes into the food processor (the juice drained off can be saved for soups or sauces) and add the tomato paste, olive oil, oregano, garlic clove, and a pinch of salt and pepper. Blend the tomato mixture for just a few seconds to make a lumpy sauce. Tip the mixture into a bowl.

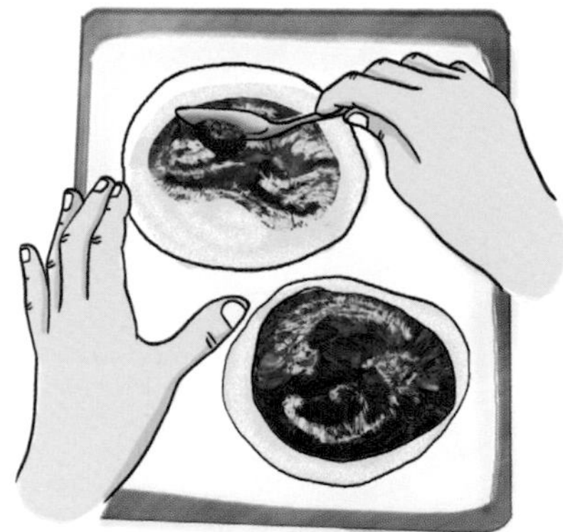

Spoon 2 tablespoons of the tomato topping onto the middle of each pizza base. Spread the tomato mixture over the base, leaving a 1-in. (2.5-cm) border of uncovered dough all around the edge.

Slice the mozzarella or pull it into long shreds. Arrange the pieces on top of the tomato sauce on the pizzas.

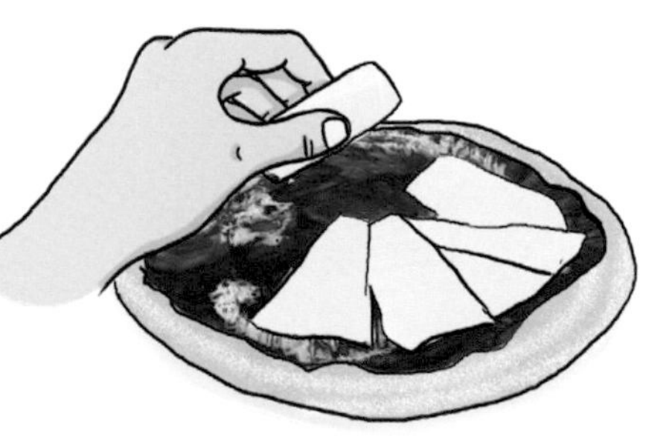

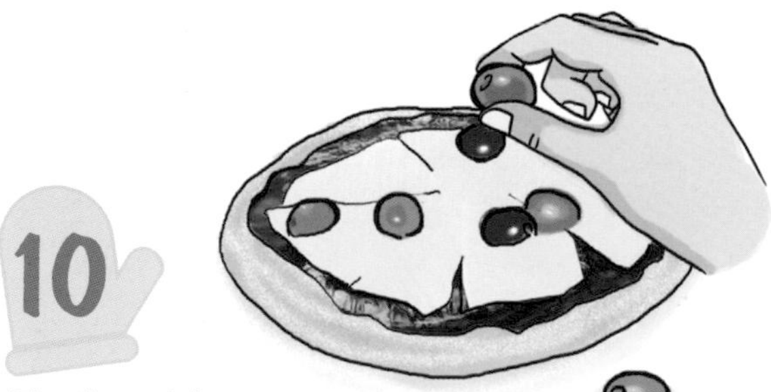

10 Finally, add as many extra toppings as you like.

Ask an adult to help you put the pizzas in the preheated oven and bake them until they are light golden and bubbling—about 15–18 minutes.

Ask an adult to help you carefully remove the pizzas from the oven, but let them cool for a couple of minutes before eating—the melted cheese can burn your mouth.

Sticky cinnamon buns

These buns use yeast to make a bread dough, but they are much richer than normal bread, because you add eggs and butter and milk. The dough is rolled up with sugar, cinnamon, and pecans or raisins then cut into slices—this makes pretty spiral buns. Eat them warm from the oven for a taste of perfection!

You will need

For the dough:

4 cups (500 g) unbleached white bread flour

1 package (¼ oz./7 g) or 2½ teaspoons active dry yeast

1 teaspoon salt

3 tablespoons superfine (caster) or granulated sugar

1⅓ cups (300 ml) milk

1 US extra-large (UK large) egg, at room temperature

3 tablespoons (45 g) unsalted butter, very soft

For the filling:

2 tablespoons (30 g) butter, very soft

1 teaspoon ground cinnamon

4 tablespoons soft light brown sugar

½ cup (60 g) pecan pieces or raisins

baking sheet

(makes 12)

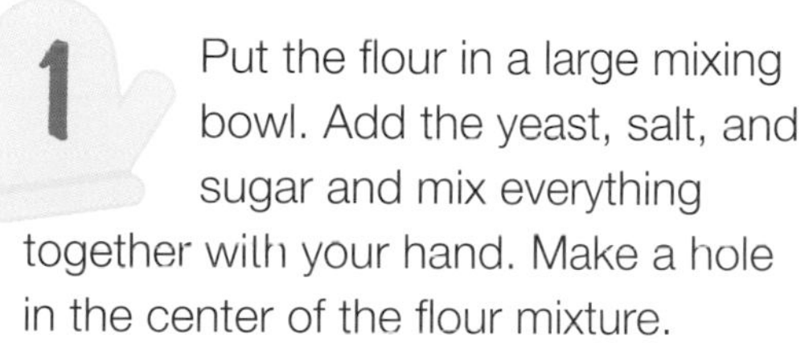

1 Put the flour in a large mixing bowl. Add the yeast, salt, and sugar and mix everything together with your hand. Make a hole in the center of the flour mixture.

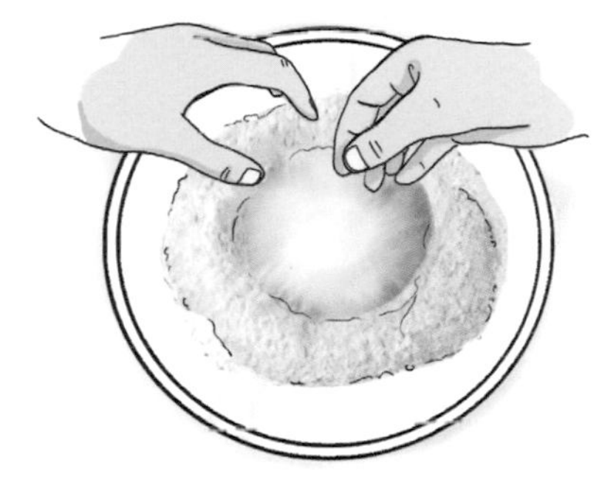

2 Ask an adult to help you warm the milk a little; either in a pan on the stove or in the microwave for about 30 seconds (see page 11). It should still be cool enough to put your finger in! Break the egg into a pitcher (jug), add the milk and beat them together with a fork. Pour the mixture into the hole in the flour and then add the butter.

3 Using your hand, slowly stir the flour into the liquid in the hollow, then work the mixture with your hand until all the flour has been mixed in. If there are dry crumbs in the bowl and the dough feels dry, add a little more milk, a tablespoonful at a time. If the dough is very sticky, add a little more flour.

4 When the mixture comes together to make a soft dough, gather it into a ball. Sprinkle a little flour over the work surface, tip the dough out of the bowl and begin to knead it. To do this, push the ball of dough down and away from you with the heel of your hand, stretching and flattening it as you push. Fold the far edge toward you. Turn the ball around half a turn and stretch the dough out again. Fold and turn again. Keep doing this until the dough is silky smooth and elastic—this will take about 5 minutes and you may need to add more flour if the dough is too sticky.

5 Put the dough back into the mixing bowl and cover with plastic wrap (clingfilm). Leave the bowl in a warm place until it has doubled in size—about 1 hour. It will take longer at normal room temperature or on a cool day.

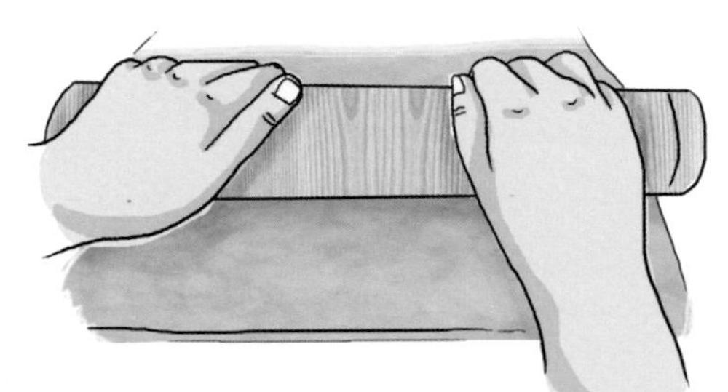

6 When it is well risen, uncover the bowl and gently punch down the dough with your fist. Sprinkle the work surface lightly with flour then tip the dough onto it. Using your hands or a rolling pin, press or roll the dough out to a rectangle about 10 x 14 in. (25 x 35 cm), with the long side toward you.

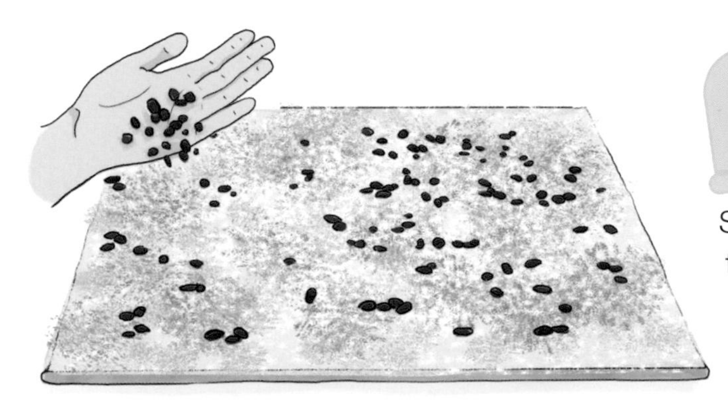

7 Spread the butter for the filling all over the dough. Mix the cinnamon and sugar together and sprinkle over the butter. Finally, scatter the nuts or raisins over the sugar and lightly press them down into the dough.

8 Roll up the dough from one of the long sides to make a long roll. Pinch the dough together all along the "seam" to seal it.

9 Put a little soft butter on a paper towel and rub it over the baking sheet to grease it.

10 Place the long roll onto a cutting board and then, using a sharp knife, mark out 12 equal-sized slices. Carefully cut the slices one by one, and lay each one flat onto the baking sheet, spacing them slightly apart.

11 Cover the sheet with a clean, dry paper towel and leave to rise again for 20 minutes. Meanwhile, ask an adult to help you turn the oven on to 425°F (220°C) Gas 7.

12 Uncover the buns, then ask an adult to help you put the sheet in the preheated oven to bake for 20 minutes, until the buns are golden brown. Ask an adult to help you remove the sheet from the oven. Use a metal spatula to lift the buns onto a wire rack to cool. They are nicest when warm, but you can eat them cold. Once they are cold, you can keep them in an airtight container and eat them within 2 days or freeze them for up to 1 month.

Irish soda bread

Irish soda bread is bread made without yeast so it is much quicker to make than normal bread, but just as delicious, especially when warm from the oven with loads of butter and jelly (jam).

You will need

vegetable oil, for greasing

2 cups (250 g) all-purpose (plain) flour

2 cups (250 g) whole-wheat (wholemeal) flour

1¼ cups (125 g) rolled oats (porridge oats)

1 teaspoon baking soda (bicarbonate of soda)

1 teaspoon fine sea salt

2 tablespoons (30 g) butter

1⅔ cups (400 ml) buttermilk (see page 10)

1 tablespoon runny honey

baking sheet

baking parchment

(makes 1 loaf)

1 Ask an adult to turn the oven on to 400ºF (200ºC) Gas 6. Put a little vegetable oil on a paper towel and rub it over the baking sheet to grease it.

2 Put the flours, oats, baking soda, and salt in a mixing bowl and stir together well. Add the butter and rub it into the flour between your fingers and thumb. (see page 9).

3 Measure the buttermilk into a pitcher (jug), add the honey, and stir them together.

Who doesn't like WARM BREAD and jelly?

4

Make a hole in the center of the flour mixture and pour in the buttermilk. Gradually stir the flour into the buttermilk until the mixture comes together into a ball of soft dough. If it feels a bit hard, add a little more milk (just add a tiny bit at a time, because you don't want the dough to go sloppy).

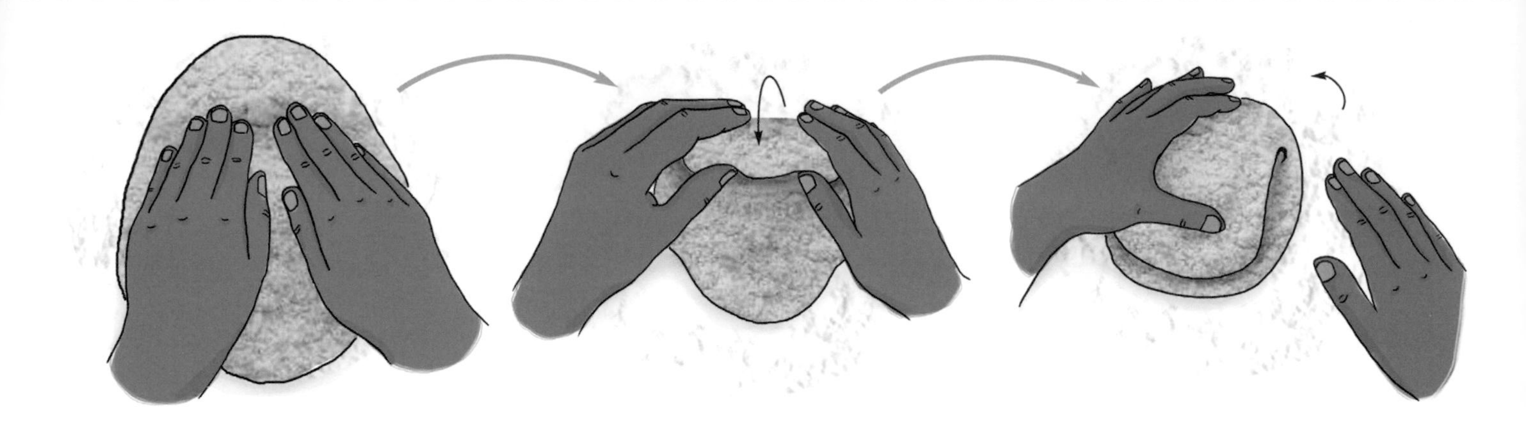

5 Sprinkle a little flour onto a clean work surface. Tip the dough onto the work surface and begin to knead it. To do this, push the ball of dough down and away from you with the heel of your hand, stretching and flattening it as you push. Fold the far edge toward you. Turn the ball around half a turn and stretch the dough out again. Fold and turn again. Keep kneading for 2–3 minutes until the dough is smooth and soft.

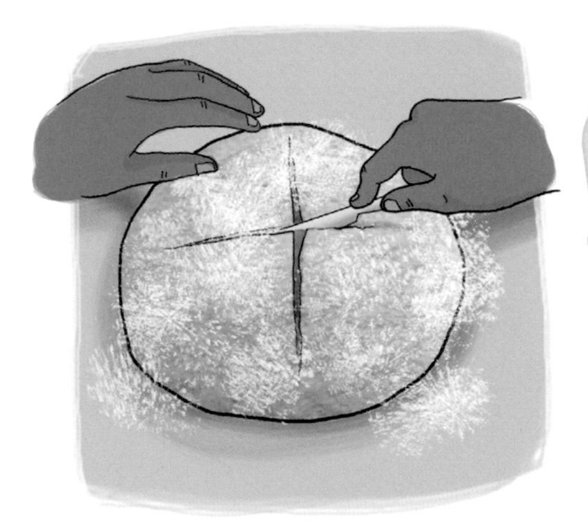

6 Shape the dough into a round loaf, sprinkle a little flour over the top, and then carefully make a large X-shaped slash in the top with a sharp knife.

7 Lift the loaf onto the baking sheet and ask an adult to help you put it in the preheated oven. Bake it for 50–55 minutes. After that time, ask an adult to take it out of the oven, then lift it up using oven mitts, and tap the bottom. Listen carefully! If it sounds hollow the bread is done. If it sounds solid it will need a little longer in the oven. When it is baked, let it cool on a wire rack.

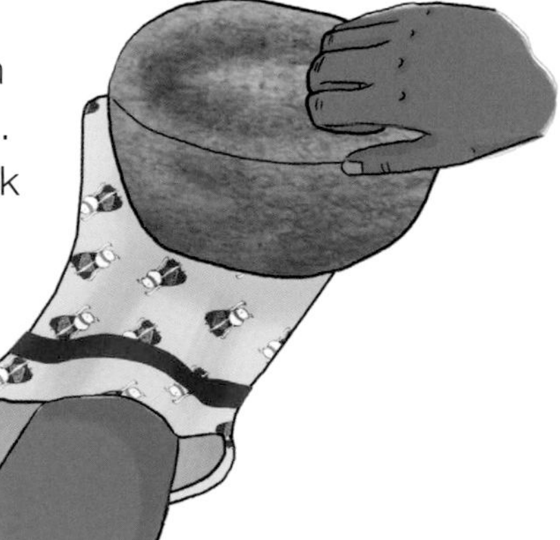

Grandma's jelly buns

These jelly-filled cookies are sturdy enough to survive life in a lunchbox, and are easy to make—the only adult help you need is with using the oven at the end. They will keep for a week in an airtight container.

You will need

1⅔ cups (225 g) self-rising (self-raising) flour

scant ½ cup (90 g) sugar, plus extra for sprinkling

1 stick (125 g) unsalted butter, chilled

1 US extra-large (UK large) egg

1 tablespoon milk

about 1 tablespoon jelly (jam)—choose your favorite flavor

2 baking sheets

(makes 16)

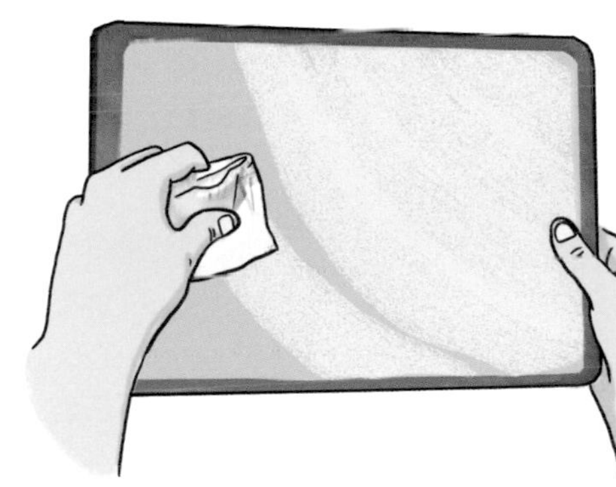

1 Ask an adult to help you turn the oven on to 400°F (200°C) Gas 6. Put a little butter on a piece of paper towel and rub it over each baking sheet to grease them.

2 Put the flour and sugar in a bowl and mix them well with your hands.

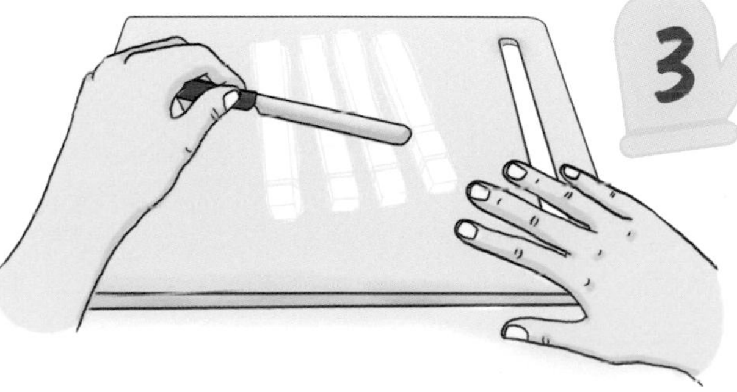

3 Cut the butter into small pieces with a round-bladed knife and add to the bowl.

Make yourself a LUNCHBOX TREAT!

4 Toss the pieces of butter in the flour so they are well coated then rub the butter into the flour, using your fingers and thumbs, until the mixture looks like fine crumbs (see page 9). Make a hole in the center of the crumby mixture.

5 Break the egg into a small bowl, pick out any pieces of shell, add the milk, and mix together with a fork.

6 Tip the egg mixture into the hole in the crumb mixture and stir the crumbs into the liquid using a round-bladed knife. It will come together to make a soft dough. If the dough is too dry and the crumbs won't stick together, add extra milk, 1 tablespoon at a time. If the dough is too wet and sticky, add 1 tablespoon extra flour until it is right.

7 Divide the dough into 16 even pieces. Roll each piece into a ball with your hands and set the balls well apart on the baking sheets.

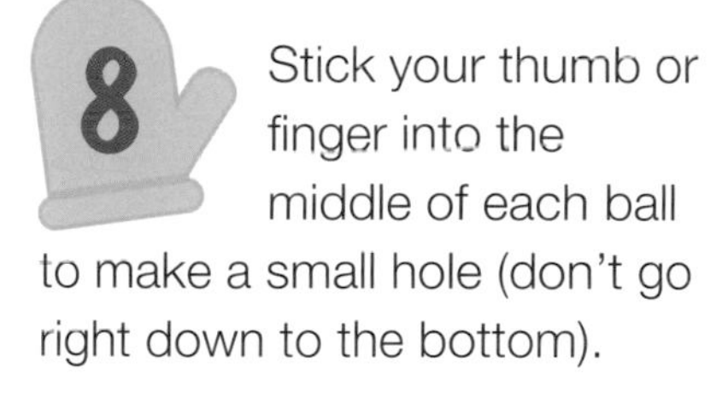

8 Stick your thumb or finger into the middle of each ball to make a small hole (don't go right down to the bottom).

9 Using a teaspoon, put a pea-size amount of the jelly (jam) in the hole, then pinch the dough back together to cover the hole (don't worry if it looks a bit messy at this point).

10 Now ask an adult to help you bake the buns. Bake for 10 minutes in the preheated oven, then turn down the heat to 350°F (180°C) Gas 4 and bake for 5 minutes more. Carefully remove the baking sheets from the oven, sprinkle the buns with a little sugar, and let them cool for 5 minutes (the jelly becomes very hot in the oven and can easily burn you). Using a spatula, transfer them to a wire cooling rack and let them cool completely.

Pick 'n' mix scones

Savory scones can be flavored with all kinds of different fillings—cheese, ham, olives, herbs, or sun-dried tomatoes. These scones make a delicious change from sandwiches to have for your lunch. You could even freeze some—take one out of the freezer in the morning, pop it in your lunchbox, and it will have thawed by lunch time.

You will need

1⅔ cups (225 g) self-rising (self-raising) flour, plus extra for kneading

1 teaspoon baking powder

3 tablespoons (45 g) butter, chilled

a handful each of only 2 of the following: cheese, fresh herbs, sun-dried tomatoes, pitted olives, or ham

½–⅔ cup (125–175 ml) milk, plus a little extra for glazing

round cookie cutter

baking sheet

(makes 8 large or 12 small scones)

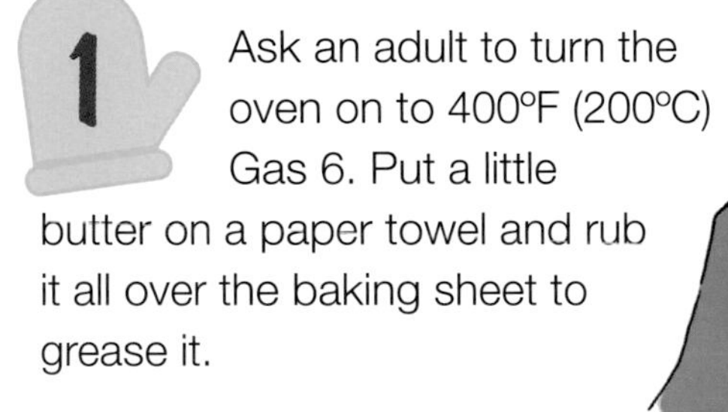

1 Ask an adult to turn the oven on to 400ºF (200ºC) Gas 6. Put a little butter on a paper towel and rub it all over the baking sheet to grease it.

2 Decide on your two favorite fillings and prepare a handful of each. If you want cheese, you need to grate it (see page 13). If you want fresh herbs, you need to chop them carefully with a sharp knife (see page 12). Olives and sun-dried tomatoes will also need cutting carefully into small pieces with a sharp knife. You could snip up ham with a pair of kitchen shears (scissors). Put your fillings to one side.

3 Put a strainer (sieve) over a large mixing bowl, and sift in the flour and baking powder.

4 Put the butter onto a chopping board and use a sharp knife to cut it into very small pieces, remembering always to cut down onto the board.

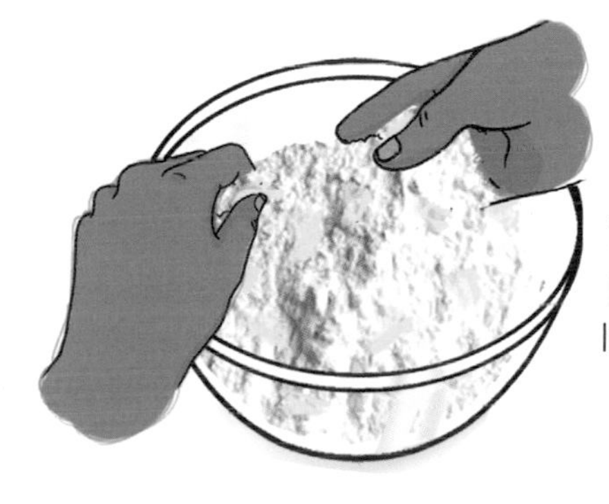

5 Add the butter to the bowl and rub it into the flour, using your fingers and thumbs (see page 9) until the mixture looks like fine breadcrumbs.

What are your **FAVORITE** fillings?

6 Stir in your two fillings, then use a round-bladed table knife to mix in the milk, one tablespoon at a time, until the mixture starts to come together into a dough. Be very careful not to add too much milk—your dough must be nice and firm and you may not need all the milk in your cup.

7 Sprinkle a little flour onto a clean work surface and then tip the dough out of the bowl. Put a little more flour on your hands and very lightly knead the mixture for about 30 seconds until it is smooth.

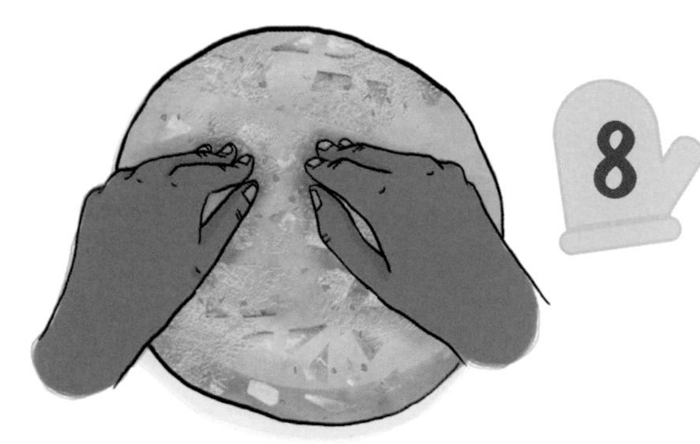

8 Make the mixture into a ball, and lightly pat it out until it is about 1¼ in. (3 cm) thick, which is quite thick.

9 Dip a round cookie cutter into a little flour and cut out the scones from the dough. Cut them as close together as you can. When you have cut as many as you can, gather up the trimmings, knead them lightly together, and pat them out—then cut some more scones. Put the scones onto the baking sheet, spaced a little apart. Use a pastry brush to brush the tops with a little milk.

Ask an adult to put the scones into the preheated oven and bake for 8–10 minutes until they are risen and golden. Ask an adult to take them out of the oven and put them on a wire rack to cool. If you want to freeze some for later, wait till they are cold, pop a few into a freezer bag or box, seal it up, and put it in the freezer.

Mini focaccias with zucchini

This bread recipe is for savory focaccia, which are little Italian style rolls. These are flavored and decorated with grated zucchini (courgette) but you could have them plain or with a sprinkle of sea salt crystals instead.

You will need

3 cups (375 g) strong (bread) flour

1 package (¼ oz./7 g) fast-acting dried yeast

salt

3 tablespoons olive oil

about ¾ cup (180 ml) warm water

2 small zucchini (courgettes)

2 large baking sheets

(makes 8)

1 Dust the baking sheets with a little flour.

2 Put the flour, yeast, and 1 teaspoon salt into a bowl and stir well with your fingers. Add 2 tablespoons of the olive oil and 1–2 tablespoons warm water. Keep mixing with your fingers, adding more warm water a little at a time, until the mixture comes together into a soft but not sticky dough (if you add too much water, add a little more flour).

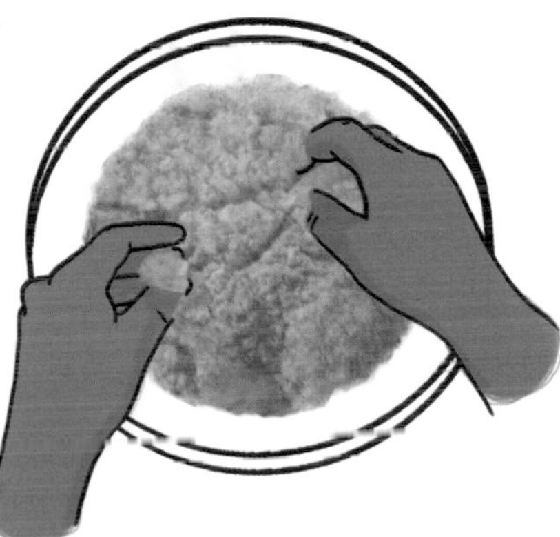

Sprinkle a little flour onto a clean work surface. Shape the dough into a ball, tip it out onto the work surface, and begin to knead it. To do this, push the ball of dough down and away from you with the heel of your hand, stretching and flattening it as you push. Fold the far edge toward you. Turn the ball around half a turn and stretch the dough out again. Fold and turn again. Keep doing this until the dough is silky smooth and stretchy—this will take 5–10 minutes and you may need to add more flour if the dough is too sticky.

4

Divide the dough into 8 pieces and knead each piece again until it is smooth. Using a rolling pin, roll each piece into a small circle just over ½ in. (1.5 cm) thick. Lay the circles, spaced well apart, on the baking sheets and cover them with plastic wrap (clingfilm). Put them in a warm place to rise for about 40 minutes, until they have doubled in size. (They will take longer if you haven't got a warm place to put them.)

Ask an adult to help you turn the oven on to 425ºF (220ºC) Gas 7.

Wash the zucchini (courgettes) and then, using a sharp knife and cutting down onto a board, trim off both ends. Now grate them carefully onto a plate using a fine cheese grater (see page 13). Sprinkle on a little salt.

7 Add the remaining olive oil to the grated zucchini and mix up well with your hands. Scatter the grated zucchini over the mini-focaccias.

8 When the oven is hot, ask an adult to help you put in the mini-focaccias and bake them for about 10–15 minutes. Ask an adult to help you take them out and test them to see if they are baked—they should be firm and golden, and sound hollow when tapped on their bottoms! Serve them warm, or let them cool on a wire rack.

CHAPTER FOUR

SAVORY MEALS AND SNACKS

Tasty bread tartlets

Sometimes you want to do some cooking, but when you look in the fridge and the pantry, you find that there are none of the ingredients you need. These little tartlets use ingredients that almost everyone will find in their kitchen: bread, milk, eggs, and frozen peas. You can also make them with different fillings, like corn and tuna.

You will need

- a little butter
- 6 slices of bread
- 3 eggs and 4 tablespoons milk (or 2 eggs and 6 tablespoons milk)
- a handful of fresh mint leaves (optional)
- 2 handfuls of frozen peas (defrosted), fresh peas, or corn kernels
- a small handful of grated Parmesan cheese

6-hole muffin pan

large, round cutter as wide as the slices of bread

(makes 6)

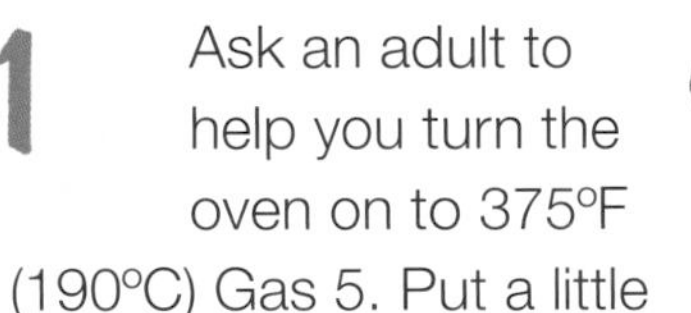

1 Ask an adult to help you turn the oven on to 375ºF (190ºC) Gas 5. Put a little butter on a piece of paper towel and rub it inside 6 of the holes in the muffin pan to grease it.

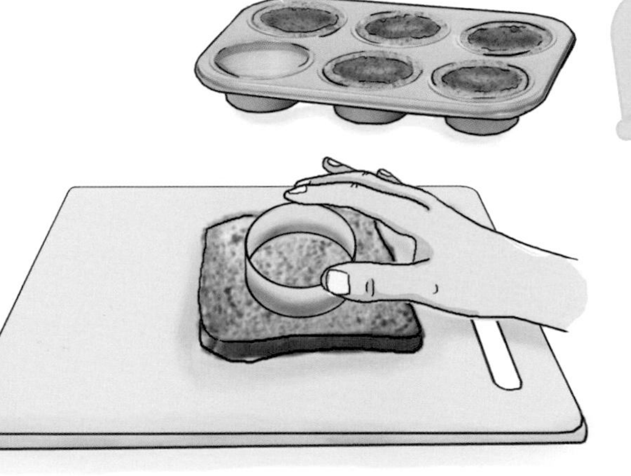

2 Lay a piece of bread on a chopping board and use the round cutter to cut out a circle of bread. Press it into the muffin pan. Do the same with the other slices of bread.

3 Ask an adult to help you put the muffin pan into the oven to bake for 5 minutes. Ask an adult to help you take the muffin pan out of the oven and let it cool.

EASY PEASY TARTLETS!

4

Break the eggs into a measuring cup (jug) and pick out any pieces of shell. Mix the eggs with a fork to break them up. Add the milk and keep mixing to blend them together.

5

If you are using mint, use scissors to snip it into small pieces and put a little into each tartlet. Now put a few peas on top—try to share them out evenly so that the tartlets have roughly the same amount.

Carefully pour the egg mixture into the tartlets, over the peas and mint—don't fill them too full as the tartlets will rise in the oven.

7

Sprinkle a little grated Parmesan over the tartlets.

Ask an adult to help you put the muffin pan back in the oven. Bake for 12 minutes, or until the filling has puffed up and the egg is cooked.

Oven risotto with tomatoes, peas, and tuna

This is an excellent one-pot meal to cook for a family supper. Try to be very organized when you make this and have everything prepared before you start cooking.

You will need

4 scallions (spring onions)

2 garlic cloves

2 x 6 oz. (175 g) cans tuna in oil or spring water

1 x 14 oz. (400 g) can chopped tomatoes with herbs

vegetable or chicken stock cubes or powder

¾ cup (115 g) fresh or frozen peas (no need to thaw if frozen)

2 tablespoons olive oil

1 cup (200 g) arborio or other risotto rice

salt and freshly ground black pepper

Parmesan cheese

a few fresh basil leaves, to garnish (optional)

medium-size heavy, flameproof, ovenproof casserole dish with lid

(serves 4–5)

Ask an adult to help you turn the oven on to 350°F (180°C) Gas 4.

Using a small sharp knife, trim off the hairy roots of the scallions (spring onions). Remember to cut down onto a board. Next, trim off the very dark green tops. Rinse the scallions in cold running water to get rid of any grit and mud. Finally cut them into thin rounds.

3 Peel off the papery skins from the 2 cloves of garlic and put them to one side.

4

Carefully open the cans of tuna. Put a colander in the sink and tip in the tuna to drain off the liquid.

5

Ask an adult to help you boil a kettle and measure out 1¾ cups (400 ml) of hot water into a measuring cup (jug). Stir in one stock cube or a teaspoonful of stock powder to make hot stock. Carefully open the can of tomatoes and measure the peas into a bowl.

6

Now that everything is prepared you are ready to begin cooking. Spoon the olive oil into the casserole dish. Set the dish on the stove and ask an adult to help you gently heat it. Using a wooden spoon, stir in the scallions. Put the garlic into a garlic crusher and crush it into the dish. Cook very gently for 1 minute.

7

Add the rice to the casserole dish and stir well. Cook gently for 1 minute, then stir in the contents of the can of tomatoes, followed by the stock and tuna. Stir well, then add the peas and a little salt and black pepper. Stir once more, then put the lid on the dish. Ask an adult to help you put the dish in the preheated oven to bake for 35 minutes.

Just before the risotto is ready, grate about 3 tablespoons of Parmesan cheese onto a plate, using the finest holes, and tear up a few basil leaves, if you have some. Then, when the time is up, ask an adult to help you remove the casserole dish from the oven. Remove the lid, and check that the rice is soft—if not put it back for a little longer. If it is cooked, scatter over the Parmesan cheese and the basil leaves. Eat immediately.

This is lovely with a salad made from green leaves and some cherry tomatoes.

A ONE-POT supper dish!

Chorizo and cheese muffins

These savory muffins are great for parties, picnics, and lunchboxes. If you eat them when they are still warm, you will find pockets of melted cheese as well as tasty bites of spicy sausage.

You will need

4 cups (500 g) all-purpose (plain) flour

2 teaspoons baking powder

a pinch of salt

freshly ground black pepper

8 oz. (225 g) Swiss cheese (such as Emmental)

4 oz. (115 g) thickly sliced chorizo sausage (or ham, or canned or frozen sweetcorn kernels)

2 US extra-large (UK large) eggs

scant stick (100 g) unsalted butter

1½ cups (350 ml) milk

12-hole muffin pan

paper muffin cases

(makes 12)

1 Line the muffin pan with the muffin cases. Ask an adult to turn the oven on to 400°F (200°C) Gas 6.

2 Set a large strainer (sieve) over a mixing bowl. Tip the flour into the strainer, then add the baking powder, salt, and a few grinds of pepper, and sift these ingredients into the bowl.

3 Using a sharp knife and cutting down onto a board, cut the cheese into small cubes. Use kitchen scissors to cut up the chorizo into pieces about the same size as the cheese.

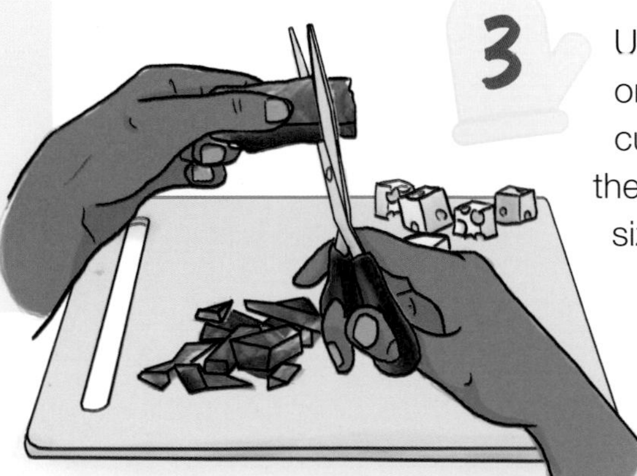

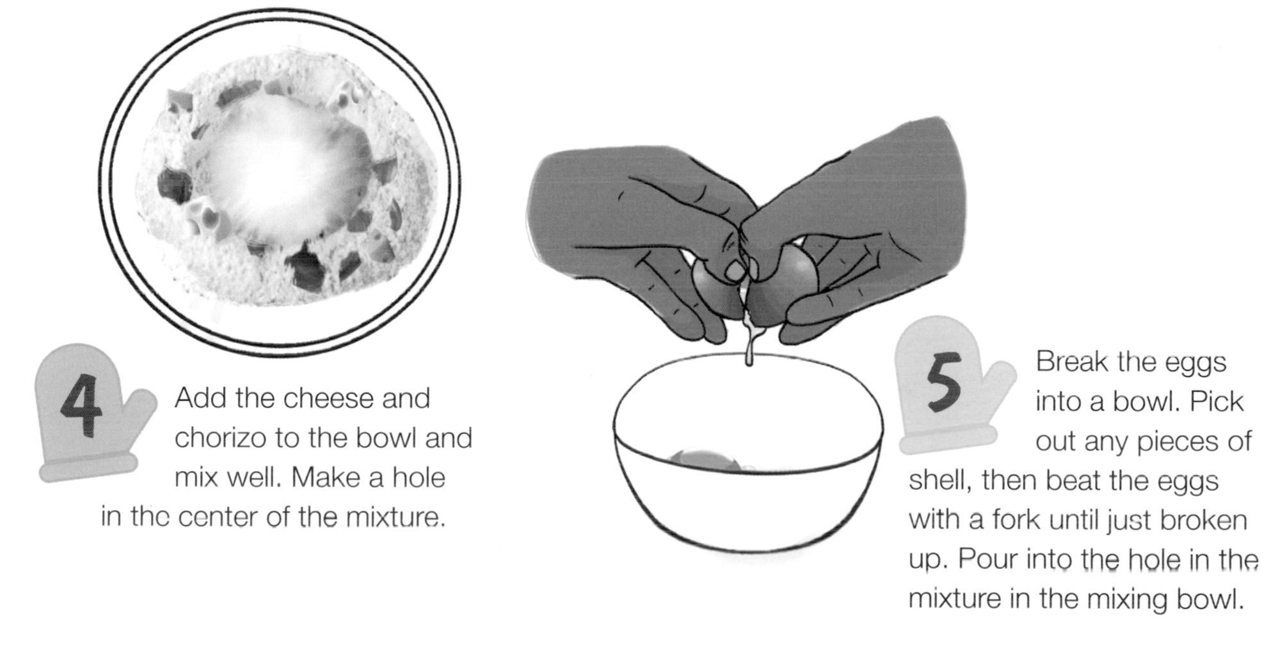

4 Add the cheese and chorizo to the bowl and mix well. Make a hole in the center of the mixture.

5 Break the eggs into a bowl. Pick out any pieces of shell, then beat the eggs with a fork until just broken up. Pour into the hole in the mixture in the mixing bowl.

6 Put the butter in a small saucepan and ask an adult to help you melt the butter over very low heat. The butter can also be melted in a microwave (see page 11). Pour the butter into the hole in the mixture. Then pour in the milk.

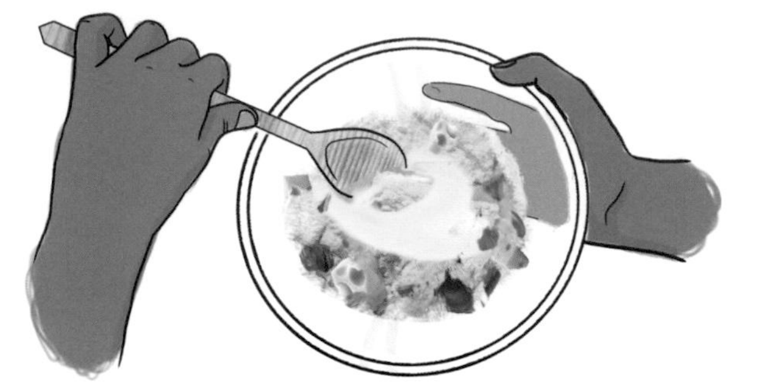

7 Mix all the ingredients together with a wooden spoon, gradually mixing the dry ingredients into the well of liquids in the center. Keep stirring to make a rough-looking mixture.

Spoon this mixture into the prepared muffin cases, making sure there is the same amount in each one. Ask an adult to help you put the muffins in the oven to bake for 30 minutes, until golden brown.

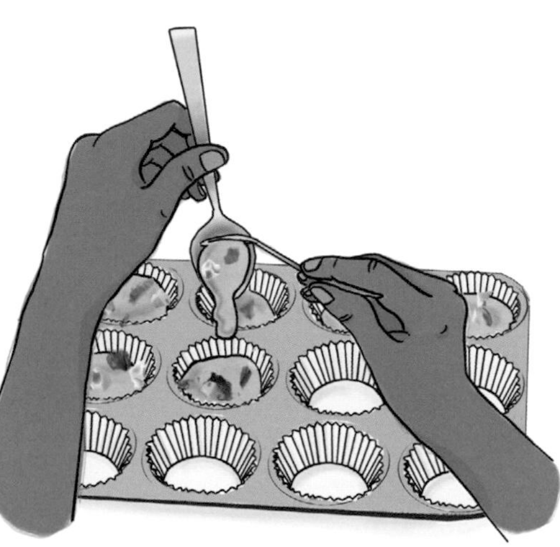

9 Ask an adult to help you remove the pan from the oven. Let it cool for a couple of minutes, then transfer the muffins to a wire rack. Eat warm or at room temperature. You can store them in an airtight container to eat the next day.

Cheese and chorizo SURPRISE!

Mini toads

Who likes eating toads? Yuk! What a thought—but you're sure to love this mini version of toad in the hole, which is a funny old-fashioned name for sausages in batter. You must work very carefully but quickly at the end of this recipe, because you need the oil to be really hot to make the batter puff up around the sausages.

You will need

¾ cup (75 g) all-purpose (plain) flour

a pinch of salt

a pinch of pepper

2 eggs

1 cup (250 ml) milk

a small bunch of fresh chives (optional)

12 breakfast link (chipolata) sausages (any type, including vegetarian)

¼ cup (60 ml) vegetable oil

large baking sheet or roasting pan

12-hole muffin pan

(makes 12)

1 Ask an adult to help you adjust the oven shelves—you will be using the middle one for the muffin pan, so make sure there is plenty of room for the batter to rise above the pan. Put a shelf under the middle one and put a large baking sheet or roasting pan on it to catch any drips. Ask an adult to help you turn the oven on to 425°F (220°C) Gas 7.

2 To make the batter, put the flour, salt, and pepper in a large bowl. Make a hole in the center.

3 Break the eggs into a bowl, pick out any pieces of shell, and add the milk. Whisk them together with a wire whisk then pour into the hole in the flour.

4 Still using the whisk, start to mix the flour into the milk and eggs, pulling in a little flour at a time. When all the flour has been mixed in, beat the batter well to get rid of any lumps.

5 Use kitchen shears (scissors) to snip the chives into the batter and stir them in. You can make the batter up to 3 hours before you start cooking.

6 Using kitchen shears again, snip the links between the sausages to separate them. If your sausages are too long, then twist each one in the middle to make two small sausages and snip through the twist to separate them. Put them to one side. Wash your hands well after handling the sausages.

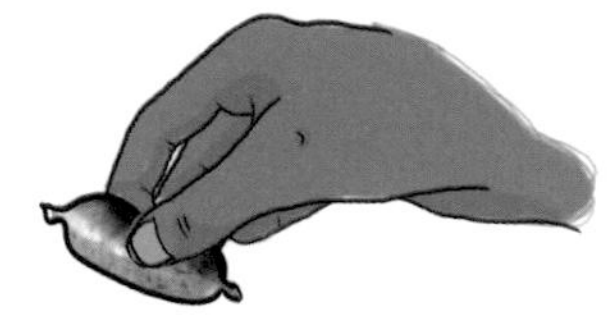

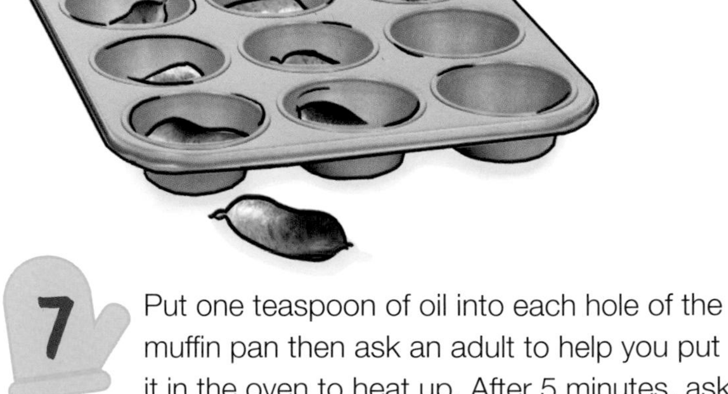

7 Put one teaspoon of oil into each hole of the muffin pan then ask an adult to help you put it in the oven to heat up. After 5 minutes, ask an adult to help you remove the pan—wear oven mitts as the pan and oil will be very, very hot—and put it onto a heatproof work surface. Carefully put one sausage into each hole, then ask an adult to help you put the pan back in the oven for another 5 minutes.

8 For the next stage you need to work quickly. Get ready by pouring or ladling the batter into a large measuring cup (jug) and stir it once or twice. Now, ask an adult to help you carefully remove the hot pan from the oven and put it onto the heatproof work surface again, then stand back (the oil can splutter), then ask an adult to help you quickly pour the batter into each hole so each one is half full.

9 Ask an adult to help you replace the pan in the oven and bake for 20 minutes until the batter is golden brown and crispy.

10 Ask an adult to help you remove the pan from the oven and lift each Mini Toad out of the pan with a round-bladed knife. Use an oven mitt to steady the pan. Eat straight away with salad, green vegetables, or baked beans.

Do you like **EATING TOADS?**

Cornmeal and sweetcorn fritters

These little fritters are made with a batter similar to that for Mini Toads (see page 111), but they are fried rather than baked. Although they don't really belong in a baking book, we've included them here as they taste so good and are such an easy supper for you to help make.

You will need

1 cup (160 g) cornmeal (or fine polenta)

¼ cup (40 g) all-purpose (plain) or whole-wheat (wholemeal) flour

2 teaspoons baking powder

¼ teaspoon paprika

½ teaspoon fine sea salt

¾ cup (200 ml) milk, plus more if needed

1 egg

2 cups (300 g) sweetcorn kernels, fresh, frozen, or canned

sunflower oil and butter

skillet (frying pan)

heatproof dish

(makes about 7)

1 In a large bowl, mix together the cornmeal, flour, baking powder, paprika, and salt.

Measure the milk into a measuring cup (jug), add the egg, and whisk until blended.

3 Pour the milk mixture into the cornmeal mixture and stir until it is well mixed together. Stir in the sweetcorn kernels.

Serve up a SIMPLE SUPPER!

4 Ask an adult to help you with all the next stages of cooking, as you will be using the stovetop (hob) and the oven. First, turn the oven on to low 225ºF (110ºC) Gas ¼ (just to keep the cooked fritters warm while you cook the others) and put a heatproof dish into the oven to warm up.

5 Put one tablespoon of oil and a small knob of butter into a large nonstick skillet (frying pan) and ask an adult to help you put it on the stove to heat up. When the oil is sizzling, ask an adult to help you pour a ladleful of the batter into the pan to make one fritter. Add one or two more ladles of batter to the pan, but space out the fritters so that they don't run into one other. Cooking fewer at a time is easier than having them too close.

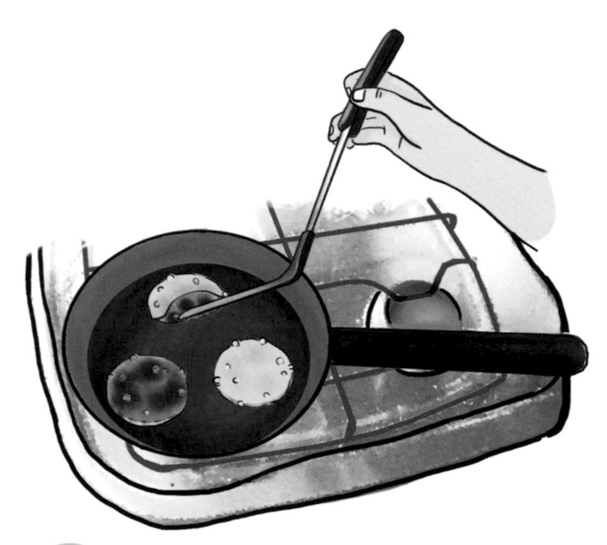

6 Cook for 3–5 minutes on one side, until each fritter has bubbles all over and, when you lift the edge with a spatula, it is brown underneath. Using the spatula, turn each one over and cook the other side until, when you peep underneath, it is golden brown on that side too.

7 Ask an adult to help you remove the fritters from the pan, drain them on paper towels, then transfer them to the heatproof plate in the oven, to keep warm while you cook the rest. Serve immediately.

Baked polenta with cheese

Northern Italians often eat polenta rather than pasta. This dish is buttery, cheesy, and delicious. The polenta comes as tiny grains, which swell when you cook it and then you can cut it into shapes and bake it. A special Italian cheese called Taleggio is used for this recipe, but you could use any cheese that melts well, instead.

You will need

1½ cups (250 g) instant cornmeal (polenta)

vegetable stock cubes or powder

6 oz. (170 g) Parmesan cheese

2 handfuls of baby spinach

7 tablespoons (100 g) butter, softened

3½ oz. (100 g) Taleggio cheese (in one piece), or other melting cheese, such as Gruyère, Cheddar, Fontina, or Emmental

sunflower oil

salt and black pepper

baking sheet

cookie cutter

large ovenproof dish

(serves 4)

First prepare all your ingredients: grate the Parmesan onto a plate using the finest grater. Wash the spinach in a colander and tear the leaves into small pieces. Measure the polenta into a measuring cup or pitcher (jug). Measure the butter onto a plate. Have the salt and pepper handy.

2 You need an adult to help you with all of the next three stages as you will be working at the stove. Pour 4 cups (1 liter) of water into a large, heavy saucepan and then ask an adult to help you put it on the stovetop (hob) and turn on the heat. When it is nearly boiling, add a stock cube or some powder, according to the instructions on the packet, to make a vegetable stock.

A cheesy ITALIAN TREAT!

3 Give the stock a stir and, when it is bubbling nicely, pour in the polenta in a steady stream with one hand, while you stir quickly all the time with a large wire whisk. (It might be easier if the adult pours while you whisk.) Do it gently so that it doesn't splash. Cook the polenta for the time recommended on the package you are using.

When the polenta is cooked and thick, remove the pan from the heat and stand it on a heatproof work surface. Use an oven mitt to hold the saucepan handle. Swap the whisk for a wooden spoon and stir in the Parmesan, spinach, a little pepper, and half the butter. Try a little on a teaspoon (making sure it's not too hot first!) and see how it tastes. Add a little salt if you think it needs it.

5 Put a little sunflower oil on a paper towel and wipe it over the baking sheet to grease it. Then ask an adult to help you pour the polenta mixture out onto the baking sheet. Smooth it over with the back of a spoon or a palette knife. Let it cool and set.

Ask an adult to help you turn the oven on to 400ºF (200ºC) Gas 6.

Cut the cooled polenta into circles using a cookie cutter—cut them as close together as possible—and lay them in the ovenproof dish. When you have cut as many as you can, push the trimmings together to cut some more.

8 Use a sharp knife to cut the cheese into little pieces; remember to cut down onto a chopping board. Dot the cheese evenly over the circles of polenta then dot over little pieces of the remaining butter.

Ask an adult to help you bake the polenta in the preheated oven for about 15–20 minutes, until the cheese is melted and bubbling.

Big pasta shells stuffed with herbs and ricotta

This is a really easy and unusual pasta dish for the whole family. It's just as tasty as lasagna, but much less trouble to make.

You will need

- 14 oz. (400 g) dried big pasta shells
- a pinch of salt
- 3 ripe tomatoes
- 1 lb. (450 g) ricotta cheese
- 2 tablespoons mixed fresh herbs (such as chives, parsley, and basil)
- 3 tablespoons olive oil
- Parmesan cheese
- a crisp, green salad, to serve

ovenproof serving dish

(serves 4)

1 Ask an adult to help you turn the oven on to 350°F (180°C) Gas 4.

2 Ask an adult to help you cook the pasta. To do this, bring a big saucepan of water to a boil and add the salt. Drop in the pasta, give it a stir, and keep the heat high until the water boils again, then turn it down a little so the water doesn't boil over the top of the saucepan—but make sure it keeps boiling.

3 Cook the pasta for the amount of time it shows on the package. Use a slotted spoon to take out a piece to test when you think it is ready (be careful not to burn your tongue). The cooked shells should be "al dente," which means not quite soft. Ask an adult to help you drain them in a colander and let them cool.

4 While the pasta is cooking, start to prepare the filling. Carefully cut the tomatoes in half, holding your hand in the bridge position (see page 12) and using a sharp knife to cut down onto a board.

5

Use a teaspoon to scoop out the seeds and the center of the tomato. Squash the tomato halves flat on the board and chop them into small pieces. Put the pieces into a bowl.

6

Carefully, using a sharp knife, chop the herbs into very small pieces (see page 12).

7

Add the herbs and ricotta to the tomatoes and stir everything together.

8

When they are cool enough to hold, take a pasta shell, place a teaspoonful of the mixture inside and put it into the ovenproof serving dish. Fill all the shells in this way and arrange them in the dish—they can be packed quite tightly.

9

Sprinkle the olive oil over the pasta making sure each piece gets some. Grate about 3 tablespoons of Parmesan (see page 13) and sprinkle this on top. Ask an adult to help you put the dish into the oven and bake for 10 minutes, until it is hot. Serve with a nice crisp, green salad.

Leek frittata

A frittata is another Italian dish, a kind of super baked omelet that you can flavor with different ingredients. This one is filled with leeks and pancetta (Italian bacon), but you could try other vegetables—zucchini (courgette), onions, mushrooms, peas, or tomatoes—and perhaps top it with grated cheese. This is another great one-dish supper that you can help to make for your family.

You will need

3 leeks

3½ oz. (100 g) pancetta (or bacon)

2 tablespoons olive oil

8 US extra-large (UK large) eggs

a few fresh chives

salt and black pepper

a crisp, green salad, to serve

round ovenproof dish, about 9 in. (23 cm) diameter

(serves 4)

1 Ask an adult to help you turn the oven on to 400°F (200°C) Gas 6.

2 Using a sharp knife and cutting down carefully onto a board, trim off the bottom of the leeks where the roots are and cut off any thick, dark leaves at the top. Then, using the bridge position for your hand (see page 12), cut the leeks in half along their length and wash them very well under a running faucet (tap) —sometimes grit can get caught between the leaves.

3 Lay the halved leeks on their flat sides on the cutting board and carefully cut them into fine slices. Scatter them over the base of the ovenproof dish.

4 Use a pair of kitchen shears (scissors) to cut the pancetta into very thin, matchstick-sized strips.

5 Scatter the pancetta pieces on top of the leeks and sprinkle the olive oil all over the dish.

6 Ask an adult to help you put the dish in the preheated oven and bake for about 15 minutes, until the pancetta is cooked and the leeks are softened.

7 In the meantime, firmly tap the eggs on the side of a bowl and pull the two halves apart with your fingertips. Pick out any pieces of shell, and beat with a wire whisk until they are very smooth. Sprinkle in a little salt and black pepper.

8 Ask an adult to help you remove the hot dish from the oven and put it on a heatproof surface. Carefully pour in the eggs, taking care not to touch the hot dish.

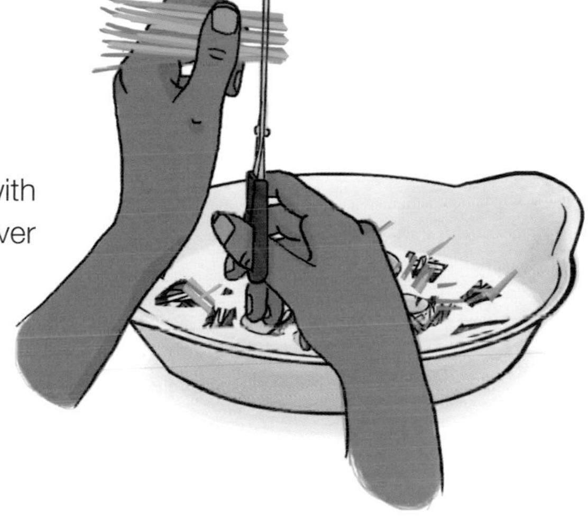

Snip the chives into pieces with kitchen shears and scatter over the frittata.

Ask an adult to help you return the dish to the oven and bake for about 20 minutes longer, until the eggs are set. Ask an adult to help you take the dish out of the oven. You can serve it warm or cold, if you prefer.

GET CRACKING on eight eggs!

Templates

You can use these templates to create stencils for the decorations on the Peanut Butter Cakes (see page 57). The recipe uses the heart stencil, but why not try pretty stars or Christmas trees instead?

Suppliers

You will probably already have most of the equipment needed for these recipes in your kitchen, but for additional bakeware supplies and, in particular, child-friendly equipment, try the following stores.

US SUPPLIERS

Foodie Kids
www.kidscookingshop.com

Fancy Flours Inc
www.fancyflours.com

Growing Cooks
www.growingcooks.com

Kids Central Kitchen
www.kidscentralkitchen.com

Kitchen Krafts
www.kitchenkrafts.com

Michaels
www.michaels.com

Sugarcraft
www.sugarcraft.com

Wilton
www.wilton.com

UK SUPPLIERS

Cakes, Cookies & Crafts
www.cakescookiesandcraftsshop.co.uk

Hobbycraft
www.hobbycraft.co.uk

John Lewis
www.johnlewis.com

The Kids Baking Store
www.thekidsbakingstore.co.uk

Lakeland
www.lakeland.co.uk

Little Chef Big Chef
littlechef-bigchef.co.uk

Spotty Green Frog
www.spottygreenfrog.co.uk

Squires Kitchen
www.squires-shop.com

Index

Acknowledgments

Key: l = left, r = right, t = top, b = bottom, c=center

Recipes
Maxine Clark: 23; Chloe Coker: 50; Linda Collister: 26, 32, 47, 57, 63, 68, 76, 82, 85, 91, 105, 108, 111; Liz Franklin: 18, 97, 117, 120, 122; Amanda Grant: 16, 36, 39, 60, 66, 94, 102; Caroline Marson: 29, 44; Annie Rigg: 20, 54, 71, 79; Laura Washburn: 88, 114

Photography
Susan Bell: 5t, 13, 37, 42, 67, 103, 104; Martin Brigdale: 15, 25; Vanessa Davies: 5bc, 9, 27, 33, 49, 83, 93, 113; Tara Fisher: 1, 17, 41, 61, 95; Lisa Linder: 2, 4b, 5bl, 6, 14, 19, 21, 55, 73, 75, 79, 81, 97, 99, 117, 119, 121, 123; Martin Norris: 4t, 43, 51; Kate Whitaker: 5br, 74, 89, 100, 115, 116, 127; Polly Wreford: 3, 7, 31, 45, 57, 59, 65, 69, 77, 87, 101, 107, 109, 110, 126

Styling
Liz Belton: 2, 4b, 21, 55, 73, 75, 79, 81; Maxine Clark/Lindy Tubby/Helen Trent: 15, 25; Amanda Grant: 5t, 13, 17, 37, 42, 61, 67, 103, 104; Amanda Grant/Jacque Malouf/Liz Belton: 1, 41, 95; Rose Hammick: 31, 45; Joss Herd/Helen Trent: 3, 7, 57, 59, 65, 69, 77, 87, 101, 107, 109, 110, 126; Lucy McKelvie/Helen Trent: 5bc, 9, 27, 33, 49, 83, 93, 113; Luis Peral-Aranda: 4t, 43, 51; Joy Skipper/Liz Belton: 5bl, 6, 14, 19, 97, 99, 117, 119, 121, 123; Sunil Vijayakar/Liz Belton: 5br, 74, 89, 100, 115, 116, 127

Cover photography
Back cover tl/bl and cover spine: Susan Bell; back cover r: Lisa Linder; front cover tl/tc: Vanessa Davies; front cover tr: Martin Norris; front cover bc: Martin Brigdale; front cover bl/br and front inside flap: Polly Wreford